SOMEWHERE OVER THE RAINBOW, I'VE LOST MY DAMN MIND

A Manic's Mood Chart

a memoir
by
Derek Thompson

www.somewhereovertherainbowthebook.com
Cover by AmyOhMy Designs

ISBN: 1467935239
ISBN 13: 9781467935234

For my family

Somewhere Over the Rainbow, I've Lost My Damn Mind

TABLE OF CONTENTS

INTRODUCTION

SESSION

DT: I've structured this nontraditional memoir into a mood chart comprised of blog entries written about the past three years of my bipolar life. I have bipolar disorder type I and am one of a lucky few to also suffer psychotic manic episodes; yeah and you thought you were having a bad day. One of the common treatment methods for this is to keep a mood chart. Seeing how probably 95 percent of the public have no idea what a mood chart is, or any other bipolar medical term for that matter, I've invited Dr. John-Paul Heathrow to join us and offer his expertise in these sessions throughout the book. Dr. John-Paul Heathrow--

JP: JP.

DT: Oh, sorry. Dr. J--

JP: *Just* JP.

DT: Ok *just* JP, how about you give us a little background about yourself and then help us out on an explanation of a mood chart?

JP: Oh, of course. I attended a superior academic institution where I received my post-doctorate in psychiatric research studies. My thesis examined the relationships between manic episode symptoms of bipolar disorder and spiritual emergency experiences to find any trends, commonalities or similarities that may exist. And I also want to make it clear from the get go that this relationship of ours must remain purely professional and platonic throughout the book, Derek Lee.

DT: Ha-ha. First off, I don't even want to know how you *already* got my middle name. And secondly, there shouldn't be too much of a problem with our relationship status, JP, because I woke up this morning still straight. So about that mood chart description?

JP: Very good, I'm glad we're on the same page. Let's see now, well, mood charts are intended to provide people with a simple way to monitor their bipolar disorder. Mood charting allows users to bring together important pieces of information such as mood state, medication levels, and stressful events. Recording this information on a chart generates a simple graph on which you can see emerging patterns that otherwise might be difficult to identify. Mood charting is a good way to record events and will help users report their mood to their doctor more efficiently.

These charts typically contain three states of mood: Depressed, Normal and Elevated. There also will be mild, moderate and severe levels of intensity within the Depressed and Elevated mood levels, while the Normal level will remain constant. Many charts represent the different moods with the colors of the rainbow, starting with violet as severely depressed and ascending to red as severely elevated.

DT: Thanks for that, JP. Obviously, I'm quite familiar with these "tools" of treating BMD[1] and unfortunately have not had much success with them in the past. But "I've never quit anything in my life except for Chinese calligraphy, my Theses 2, Kangaroo Anatomy, Toe Photography, Booger sculpture and masturbation; well, maybe not masturbation, but give me a break, it's the only thing I'm good at.--"

JP: Wait a tick. Isn't that quote from *Bio-Dome?*

DT: Why yes it is and I must say I'm already thoroughly impressed with ya JP. We're going to get along great. But back to my original point which is why I refuse to quit on mood charts, which brings us to *Somewhere Over the Rainbow, I've Lost My Damn Mind: A Manic's Mood Chart.*

This book doesn't really have a linear storyline that's organized through chapters; nope, none of that traditional memoir shit here. Instead, the book is broken up into the three sections of a mood chart: Depressed, Normal and Elevated. The Normal section is constant and will be represented by the color green; while within the Depressed and Elevated sections, there will be three intensity levels of mild, moderate and severe, with three corresponding colors of the rainbow representing those moods/ entries. The colors will start at violet for severely depressed, ascending up through the rainbow to red for severely elevated. You know what? If this is starting to get a little confusing, please see page 4 and the table titled "Manic's Mood Chart." Oh, and you'll

1   Please see page 5 for the Glossary *de* Slang for all of your translation needs

also be able to find the transcripts from my sessions with JP after each entry, similar to this first one you're reading now. Last but not least, this nontraditional memoir is also not organized in chronological order with a beginning, middle and end--

JP: Thankfully. That's *so* been done before.

DT: Ha-ha, exactly. JP knows what I'm talking about. So basically, what that means is that you can read the book from beginning to end, or feel free to flip through it and read the entries in any order you'd like. I hope you enjoy the ride.

MANIC'S MOOD CHART

Color	Mood	Intensity	Pages
Violet	Depressed	Severe	14–24
Indigo	Depressed	Moderate	25–37
Blue	Depressed	Mild	38–58
Green	Normal	Normal	59–132
Yellow	Elevated	Mild	133–159
Orange	Elevated	Moderate	160–182
Red	Elevated	Severe	183–216

Glossary *de* Slang

#truestory#fact#honesty: Follow me on twitter @e4d01rok (sometimes I say funny shit).

A

A-Town: The Durty Durty, Hotlanta, the ATL, or Atlanta, Georgia.

AT&Tizzle: AT&T (derr).

Atroxtheatrophobia: I made this word up to mean a fear of scary movies. Don't act like you're not impressed.

Awesomeville: "Someplace warm. A place where the beer flows like wine. Where beautiful women instinctively flock like the salmon of Capistrano. I'm talking about a little place called Awesomeville." –Some may think this place is Aspen from the *Dumb and Dumber* quote, but it's not.

B

Big Body Beamer: Black BMW X5 with 20s (Naw, they were 18s but I kept 'em clean!- Totally ganked that from Day-Day in *Next Friday*).

Big D: Depression

BMD: Bipolar Manic Depression

Boob tube: Baby-sitter, box, idiot box, receiver, small screen, telly, tube, TV, TV set

Boot: "I say hurl. If you blow chunks and she comes back, she's yours. But if you spew and she bolts, then it was never meant to be." –Wayne Campbell, *Wayne's World*

Brit: What I call Britney Spears. Oh, you didn't know we were on a nickname basis? Neither does she.

Browntown: Springtucky, The Field, or Springfield, Ohio. Recently named the third worst city to live in The Gallup-Healthways Well-Being Index; so they got that going for them, which is nice-I once saw Bill Murray in a bar, he's tall and this is also his quote from *Caddy Shack*.

BTW: By the way. Really, you didn't know this one? My grandma texted me this yesterday.

C

Chubs: 103 years and counting!!!! Yeah I'm talking to you Cubbies and your World Series drought, ha-ha.

Cord snakes: I really, really hate snakes so of course I hallucinated that power cords in my apartment were snakes when I was manic (trippy).

"Cornfield locked": Similar to landlocked except with a shit ton of corn around you

COSI: Center Of Science and Industry. COSI is all about mind-blowing fun, providing opportunities to play, explore, discover and learn together. Who wouldn't want to go on a date here? I mean, they also have Astronaut Ice Cream, badass, I know.

Cap'n Geech and the Shrimp Shack Shooters: *The Wonders'* musical influence. Hint: Tom Hanks directed, wrote and starred in this movie.

Child please: "Is like a nice way to tell someone: man, fuck you!"-Chad Ochocinco

City of Wind: Common's nickname for Chicago I'm "borrowing," hopefully without any kind of financial or other negative consequences. I actually paid for your music online, Common. Can we call it even?

Cycling: Going from dancing to crying in about a second flat and then back to dancing before my eyes can dry, only to end up right back at crying. Repeat.

D

d01roK: The manic me.

DayWasted: Drunk with the sun still up. I totally stole this from Olivia Munn; Olivia if you're upset about it, we can talk about it over dinner.

Derr: A sarcastic response to an obvious question, inspired by a quote from *Saving Silverman*. Yes, I know, I have shitty taste in movies.

Danke: It's German for something . . .

DIA: Denver International Airport (or the Emerald City when I'm manic).

"Drop Inches From Your Waistline While Only Partially Losing Your Mind"
!!!Investment opportunities still available!!!

Drunky Brewster: Similar to DayWasted (my dinner offer still stands Olivia) except the drunkenness carries over, into and through the night.

Dumbfoundedness: A state of complete and utter confusion characterized by symptoms of stupidity and numbness.

E

.e4: www.e4-d01rok.blogspot.com. Where this all got started.

Effin': The F-Bomb, Firetruck, Frick, Frack, Fudge, or Fuck(in).

El Doc: Cincinnati doctor in charge of the study I participated after he found me manic as shit in the psych ward. The study was using a MRI machine to compare brain images of people in manic episodes with ones when they are out of the mania and on lithium; good people.

F

Fag: A cigarette (I assure you).

G

Ganked: To borrow something without any intention of returning it, OK it's stealing.

Gainer: A badass back somersault while jumping forward and capping it off with a can opener or sleeper (diver's preference) into a pool.

Gonosyphilaherpaids: It burns, burns *real* bad when you pee. I mean, I've only read about the symptoms.

"Gournal": "Don't you mean journal?" "Yeah, whatever. I guess I'm not all smart like you."-*Wet Hot American Summer* but I'm sure you all already knew that obscure and random pop-culture reference from Paul Rudd and Elizabeth Banks.

Grass fairy: Name I was called for playing soccer while growing up (not that I still have a complex about it or anything).

H

Hole(d): A mood state in which the mania grabs me and won't let go, spinning me down into a hole of despair in my mind where I fight it off over a matter of minutes (usually in the bathroom).

I

I kid, I kid: It's a joke; seriously, chill out. You're kind of acting like Eminem at the MTV VMA's in 2002.

J

J. Crew U: "The Miz," Walter "Wally" Szczerbiak, and according to eye witnesses "Not so big" Ben all walked the campus of Miami University (of Ohio).

Jeep Wave: It's a Jeep thing. You wouldn't understand.

K

K: Abbreviation for kindergarten and also the only grade I ever repeated (well I also was a fifth year senior at Witt but graduating college in four years is like leaving the party at ten).

KY: Kentucky Y'all!

L

M

Man Card: I could tell you, but then again men don't gossip.

MD 20/20: An American fortified wine, often called by its nickname, Mad Dog. MD 20/20 has an alcohol content that varies by flavor from 13 percent to 18 percent. Most of the 18 percent varieties are discontinued, although Red Grape is reportedly available in 18 percent ABV. The MD actually stands for its producer, Mogen David. Originally, 20/20 stood for 20 ounce @ 20 percent alcohol. Currently, MD 20/20 is not sold in 20 ounce bottles or at 20 percent alcohol by volume. (Definitely ganked this off Wikipedia.).

Meow: I bet you I can say meow ten times in this book (meow, meow, meow; told ya). You probably won't get this or think it's funny unless you've seen *Super Troopers.*

Mojo: "Mojo: The libido. The life force. The essence. The right stuff. What the French call a certain... I don't know what." –Dr. Evil

Monkey: The baby of the family and my youngest brother (four years younger).

My Blunder: It's easier to watch *Observe and Protect* than for me to try and explain this and unintentionally that movie also has a bipolar character, funny how things sometimes work out.

N

NBD: No Big Deals

NKOTB: New Kids On The Block (Donnie in *Sixth Sense* still gives me the creeps).

O

P

Peeps: These are my people.

Poncho: The middle child of the family and my younger brother (two years younger).

Q

Que-evs: It means whatever but said with a lot more of an attitude.

R

Radical: Interchangeable with Totally Boss.

(Radio Edit): My attempts to not get sued for slander, or libel, or whatever.

Re-dunk-u-luss: I'm not even really sure what I meant by that.

S

Sis: My Southern belle sister who really isn't in my family but when we were Drunky Brewsters in the A-Town bars we told everyone we were. "I mean look, we have brown hair *and* eyes, don't you see the family resemblance?!"

Slamming Hot Body Trainer: No idea her name but she was the real reason I went to the gym.

South Chuck: My hometown of South Charleston, Ohio.

Southside!: The psych ward unit in University Hospital, Cincinnati.

Stubby: My dad.

T

T.A.N.: Tough As Nails

TBC . . .: To Be Continued . . .

The Nasty: The Queen City, The Nati, Porkopolis, or Cincinnati, Ohio.

The Sticks: Way out in the middle of nowhere. I'm talking *Deliverance* spooky folks.

Three Sheets: I'm like 50 percent sure this show is now called *Drinking Made Easy* and would be 100 percent positive either way if I just googled it.

Tommy Toughnuts: Similar to truck nuts but not quite as cool. Actually it just means you think you're a badass but I really wanted to reference truck nuts in the book (weird I know).

Totally Boss: Interchangeable with Radical.

TPO: Team Positively Optimistic. That was the actual name I gave to my team at AT&Tizzle when I mentored apprentices. They loved it or at least acted like they did.

Trippy: Psychedelic; accompanied by or producing distorted visual or sound effects similar to those associated with psychedelic drugs (or so I've been told).

U

V

V-Card: My innocence and/or virginity some random girl took from me my senior year spring break. Yeah, I was a late bloomer in high school but at least I didn't pay for it.

W

Witt: Witt Bubble, Streaking the Hollow, Tiger Up, or Wittenberg University.

X

Y

Yank: What the UGA fans in my section yelled at me (with a few expletives as well) when they found out I didn't know there were "no jeans on game day!" because I was wearing jeans and from Ohio at a Bulldog football game.

Z

DEPRESSED
(VIOLET, INDIGO, BLUE)

ABSTRACT:

THE DEPRESSED SECTION OF THE MOOD CHART ENCOMPASSES THREE LEVELS OF INTENSITY. VIOLET REPRESENTS THE SEVERE AND MOST EXTREME LEVEL. IN THIS STATE, THERE IS SIGNIFICANT IMPAIRMENT WITH AN INABILITY TO WORK. NEXT IS INDIGO THE MODERATE LEVEL WITHIN DEPRESSION, HIGHLIGHTED BY SIGNIFICANT IMPAIRMENT BUT WITH THE ABILITY TO WORK. THE FINAL LEVEL IS BLUE, THE MILD LEVEL OF DEPRESSION, IN WHICH THE PERSON IS WITHOUT SIGNIFICANT IMPAIRMENT AND ABLE TO WORK. THIS SECTION CONSISTS OF EIGHTEEN ENTRIES, WITH BLUE CONTAINING THE MOST ENTRIES AT EIGHT.

VIOLET

(DEPRESSED SEVERE MOODS,
SIGNIFICANT IMPAIRMENT,
UNABLE TO WORK)

KEY TERMS: FFA, HOMECOMING, BIG D, ALONENESS
Submitted on 3/31/10
Violet

Growing up in South Chuck, there were a couple of things that absolutely intimidated the buh-Jesus out of me. The first was the Future Farmers of America Tractor Day at school. Now, for those of you who have not had the ultimate pleasure of participating in an FFA Tractor Day, I'll attempt to explain this nightmare scenario. Because the FFA-is a nationally chartered high school organization, they get to wear these really sharp felt-like blue and gold jackets, and they are afforded certain privileges throughout the year. One of these privileges is similar to Spirit Week for Homecoming, only I didn't get threatened by my date's stepdad with his watch and stepdaughter's safe return speech and "fear tactic" like I did on Homecoming. On the final day of the week they have Tractor Friday, when they allow the students to drive tractors to school. No, really, I have the pictures to prove it.

(I told you I had pictures)

The hallways of the school were filled with cowboy hats (I never understood this because I've never seen a ranch in South Chuck), Wranglers (had their advantages when worn by a select few young ladies), Lacers (boots, I think), the smell of tobacco, and then me, all during FFA week leading up to the Tractor Day on Friday. Of course I was going to be driving a tractor on Friday because I was supposed to be a farmer or something, and I knew I'd get the smallest tractor. I just had that feeling; plus, I didn't know how to drive tractors. My younger brother was driving a beast of machinery that had twelve tires and barely fit under the power lines stretching across the road. My tractor was the infant baby brother to Poncho's. No matter how much smoke I blew out the pipe and how much I revved my Massey, it just didn't matter. I was still intimidated by FFA Tractor Day.

I preferred riding in the semi, when we were either hauling to the elevator or coming from the fields. I enjoyed it so much because I didn't have to do anything and could sit back and enjoy the ride. This would backfire from time to time, when I dozed off only to wake up alone. The truck had stopped, the cab was empty, and it was dead silent. That feeling of utter aloneness was a feeling I didn't like so much.

When I was recovering from manic episode uno, I went through some deep depression that took my disdain for aloneness and amplified it. I was a few months out of the hospital when this started to happen, and it got so bad that I would pray to not wake up the next day. I saw no point to anything. I've been told depression usually follows manic episodes (I think of it as a counterbalance to being so high) and after my last episode in The Nasty I wanted so badly to not feel the effects of depression again. No such luck.

The feelings of aloneness, inadequacy, worthlessness, and all their cousins have showed up again, and I still don't like them so much. Depression makes me question why all this happened, why was I given BMD and to begin to regret that it happened and feel sorry for myself. I knew the Big D was coming this time around, so I was sort of ready for these feelings, but I was no match for them in the end, really. It takes all my energy and focus to fight them off, and that unfortunately has consequences in other aspects of my life. It makes me feel as if it's not fair, and I envy others around me whose problems I wish I had.

But I can't remember when I've encountered anything in life that was truly fair. If everything was fair and even, where would I find the drive to better myself? I'd be living in a boring, predictable world. I'd rather live in a world that makes me fight for everything, because when I finally get it, there will be nothing sweeter--well, maybe an FFA Tractor Day where I drive the beast.

SESSION

JP: You've mentioned the feeling of aloneness in your depression. Did you experience any other symptoms such as decreased energy, fatigue, lethargy, diminished activity, insomnia or hypersomnia, loss of interest in pleasurable activities or social withdrawal?

DT: Yeah, I experienced just about all of these symptoms. After my first manic episode, I was depressed for around three or four months, so I obviously experienced more symptoms then. Now I'm usually able to come out of depression within a couple of months. But those months do suck.

JP: Yes. Of the over two million people in the U.S. with bipolar disorder, nearly two-thirds have chronic issues with depression and its symptoms throughout their lives.

DT: I couldn't do it; those people are way stronger than me.

KEY TERMS: DISAPPOINTMENT, WOLVERINE, MY FIRST DATE, DRIVE-INS
Submitted on 6/24/10
Violet

I started writing this blog a little over a year ago, and to say my life has changed since then would be an understatement. When I started the blog, I thought it would be my release, my therapeutic way of handling the seemingly unfair and ridiculous hand I was dealt. Since then, I've been through another manic episode, got hospitalized again, fought depression, moved to the

City of Wind, started a great internship, quit said internship, and am now planning a move back to Ohio. I'm not sure if this is helping, but it's about the only thing in my life that's not disappointing at this point.

The past year kind of reminds me of my first date. Yes, I was a freshman before I got a date and yes, it was a blind date and yes, I was set up and yes, it was as pathetic as it sounds. Just as this past year began, so did my date; I was filled with enthusiasm, optimism, excitement and all-around happiness. My best friend at the time (we'll call him Wolverine for no apparent reason other than I watched *Van Helsing* last night, on ABC Family mind you, and Jack Hughman was in it and he was also the Wolverine; this is how my mind works) talked me into going on a date with his girlfriend's best friend. I was beside myself for a number of reasons. One, I was only a freshman and they were sophomores. Two, I had a bowl cut (enough said), and three, we were heading to the drive-in. Yes, we had drive-ins where I grew up, and yes, I thought it was kind of a big deal at that time to go to one with a girl.

Wolverine was trying to get me pumped up for the date the whole way to pick up the girls, giving me confidence that I in no way deserved. I mean, I was a soccer-playing, bowl-cut, five-one, 105-pound farm boy who had never even had a girlfriend, and this girl was older, way hotter, talked into this by her friend, and a cheerleader from a rival school. If I'd had any sense at all, I would have bailed- but I liked to live life on the edge.

We showed up at the house, and the first things I noticed about my date were that she definitely didn't want to go and she was way out of my league. I tried to say hello to her mom and Wolverine's date, but my voice cracked, not once but twice We managed to get out of the house, where I left behind any semblance of dignity, and made our way to the drive-in. Being the gentleman that I am, I hid in the trunk to save the five-buck admission (but now I'm pretty sure back then it was pay by the carload, which means I got punk'd on that one) and at least become the funny guy. The movie, well, I couldn't tell you about the movie. I was too impressed watching Wolverine cuddle with his girl and somehow manage to flirt with my date. I was in awe of these moves.

In the end the date was a total disaster and a disappointing time in my life. I never went on another date with said girl as

Wolverine began dating her shortly after (that's what I got for having a hotter date than his girlfriend). I surely didn't believe I was going to make any headway with the older, more attractive, and cooler cheerleader, but I didn't think I'd get punk'd in more ways than one. Maybe that's a fault of mine that others can relate to: I can have too-high ambitions. I dream that everything will work out just right for me and that my moves in life are orchestrated in a manner destined for success. The reality is that just like my first date, this past year was built up entirely too high in my head. This makes it so much more disappointing when I don't succeed.

I have been struggling (to say the least) these past couple of weeks, dealing with the disappointment of my mania coming back and having to start over. But I do realize that I can't let this past year get me down, though it has been a huge bitch. Just like if my first date had been a success, then I more than likely wouldn't have experienced a lot of things in this world (Qantas Flight Attendant, you know what I'm saying) that have been unbelievable.

SESSION

JP: I think you're showing outstanding awareness of your situation here, Derek, and it's one of many essential concepts to have when living with bipolar disorder. A few others include:

- **Perspective:** Depression and manic depression often follow cyclical patterns. Although you may go through some painful times and it may be difficult to believe things will get better, it is important not to give up hope.

- **Personal responsibility:** It's up to you to take action to keep your moods stabilized. This includes asking for help from others when you need it, taking your medication as prescribed and keeping appointments with your health-care providers.

- **Self-advocacy:** Become an effective advocate for yourself so you can get the services and treatment you need, and make the life you want for yourself.

- **Hope:** With good symptom management, it is possible to experience long periods of wellness. Believing that you can cope with your mood disorder is both accurate and essential to recovery.

- **Education:** Learn all you can about your illness. This allows you to make informed decisions about all aspects of your life and treatment.

- **Support:** Working toward wellness is up to you. However, support from others is essential to maintaining your stability and enhancing the quality of your life.

DT: I really get the feeling you're simply quoting this stuff from a site like www.helpguide.org/mental/bipolar_disorder_self_help.htm.

JP: My resources are none of your concern. The material is what matters.

KEY TERMS: GROUP THERAPY, NEWCOMER, KNIGHTS TEMPLAR, IDENTITY
Submitted on 10/16/10
Violet

"Hi everybody, my name is Dave and I'll be leading the group today. I wanted to welcome everyone back and send out a warm welcome to our newcomer. Once again, please feel free to share as much or as little as you like, but please do have respect for the others in the group. Tonight, I want to concentrate on what irritates or angers you the most when it comes to dealing with bipolar disorder. Is there anyone one who would like to start things off? . . . Oh, great, our newcomer. Go ahead, but before you start just let everyone know your name and background."

"Oh, OK, well my name is Derek and I was diagnosed in early 2008. I have had two psychotic manic episodes requiring hospitalization since 2008, and they are mostly characterized by hallucinations, delusional thinking, and feelings of grandiosity. I hate it when my BMD takes away my personality.

"I have been through adversity in my life just as so many others have, and even more will have to in the future, but nothing could have prepared me for this. My entire life, I was under the belief that if you work hard, do the right things, keep your head down, punch the clock, and take pride in yourself and your work, eventually it will pay off. I was doing just that. I studied in school and worked hard enough to get into the college of my choice. I may have slacked a tiny bit in college, the whole five-year thing, but I got a great apprenticeship for a prominent telecom company and was looking forward to working my way up the ladder after graduation.

"I had spent from mid 2005 to 2008 getting my ass kicked but learning as much and working as hard as possible. I was looking towards the future, and the life I had been striving so hard to achieve was a mere two weeks away in California. Then I became convinced I was chosen by the Knights Templar to protect a secret that could change the course of history. I was manic for the first time.

"I should have been packing up my belongings for the move, securing an apartment in San Jose, tying up loose ends at my job and familiarizing myself with my new business in Silicon Valley. Instead, I spent my time avoiding the 'all-seeing eye in the sky' and decoding governmental, or "Freemason," symbols throughout the city of Denver. I 'pushed' my friends towards the light and 'shielded' them from the dangers of the other side. I solved the equation of life--sorry, I'm not quite ready to give up that secret yet--and 'time traveled' into my primal ancestors.

"As nutty as this sounds, the really crazy thing, pun intended there, is that even after experiencing all that my mania has to throw at me, I still do not fear it; I fear and hate my depression and its aftereffects. It's my depression that consumes me whole and pushes everything away from me. It is one mean son of a bitch that fights any way but fair. The harder I work, the deeper I fall. I begin to lose my personality and identity as all my energy is focused on fighting back the darkness inside me, the twisted thoughts that take me from reality into a world filled with emptiness, loneliness and worthlessness. I barely smile or laugh and forget what happiness feels like. I lose my identity and that is what I hate the most: trying so hard yet still not being myself."

SESSION

JP: Sharing in a group atmosphere can be a very helpful resource when fighting depression. If you're uncomfortable sharing with others but still would like to get something off your mind, a bipolar or depression chat room can be a safe, anonymous place to share.

DT: No doubt about it. Here are a few of my favorite posts I found on a random message board about depression just now:

- "For me being depressed means you can spend all day in bed, and still not get a good night's rest."

- "Depression is the inability to construct a future."

- "If depression is creeping up and must be faced, learn something about the nature of the beast: You may escape without a mauling."

KEY TERMS: CRUCIFIX, SUICIDAL THOUGHTS, ABILIFY, "MEDICINE"
Submitted on 4/15/11
Violet

I was sitting on our couch in my mom's house back in high school. Mom was in the kitchen making breakfast, and my stepdad struck up a conversation with me. My parents appeared and sounded normal, but something was off, something I couldn't quite put my finger on. Something just wasn't right.

I made my way down our hallway, past our giant oval-windowed front door, and headed upstairs. Halfway up, my brother was kneeling on the stairs, praying, and this struck me as completely out of the ordinary. At the top of our stairs, I spotted a crucifix that I'd never seen. Something was definitely wrong.

I entered my parents' room, and they chased after me, yelling at me not to go into the closet. Their familiar outward appearances slowly morphed away. I found my grey plastic storage box in their closet and opened it up. All my past sentimental belongings were inside, and I dug to the bottom where I found a letter from my girlfriend in Atlanta, still folded up exactly as she had given it to me when I had left for Denver. I took it and walked hastily downstairs, past my parents, the crucifix, my kneeling brother, and the giant oval-windowed front door. Only to stop suddenly as a message appeared on the window, just like when I was a kid and would breathe on it and steam it up and write messages, except now it read:

God loves you

It's about at this point that I woke up. Good thing, because shit was getting weird.

I was visiting my sis when this dream occurred in November 2008, about six or so months after my first manic episode. The tremors (my fancy word for my lingering manic symptoms after the episode) had passed, and now I was dealing with depression for the first time in my life (and not very well if I say so myself). I was an overmedicated zombie on Abilify and Depakene and trying to deal with the side effects of my "medicine." BTW, am I the only one who thinks a "medicine" that has a side effect of making you want to kill yourself probably shouldn't be called a medicine at all?

So I had this dream, and a few interesting things occurred, in real life this time. First, I had been struggling with back pain at this time; it seems I keep a lot of stress back there. When I woke up, the pain was gone, and stayed gone. I had a sudden realization that I could quit my "meds" and that I probably should, which I did, and it probably was a good call. The whole suicidal thoughts thing, remember? Those two things were interesting, to say the least, but I found the letter more intriguing, most likely because I had just recently discovered it during my move.

After smelling it for a few seconds or maybe a little longer (weird, I know, but it still smells like her, and damn she smelled good) I opened it up, sat down, and read about the guy I used to be. I think the part that grabbed me the most was when she mentioned that I wasn't the type of guy who wears his emotions on his sleeve, or even talks about them. I stopped reading for a second and tried to take that in, because now I'm totally opposite (mood disorder, blog, sharing my crazy emotions with the world, you get the gist). I'm still trying to process it, but I think it's a good thing, this change in me, but I could have done without the crazy dreams (nah, I like them, too).

SESSION

JP: You mentioned suicidal thoughts here; did those ever escalate to any kinds of actions?

DT: Yeah, unfortunately, a little before I had the dream mentioned in the entry above. There was one time I actually had the pills in my mouth and enough stockpiled on the counter beside me to finish myself off.

JP: What made you not do it?

DT: I just couldn't do that to my family.

INDIGO

(DEPRESSED MODERATE MOODS,
SIGNIFICANT IMPAIRMENT, ABLE TO WORK)

KEY TERMS: CARHARTTS, EL DOC, HE-MAN, FOUNDING FATHERS
Submitted on 1/27/10
Indigo

Where I come from, Carhartts, Lacers, FFA and tractors are cool. The crops, the weather, and debating township issues are the main topics of conversation. Dip, chaw, chew and spitters are signs of social acceptance. Everyone is your neighbor, and in times of crisis, help isn't asked for; it's already been given. Where I come from may not be perfect, but its home and I've begun to realize that just maybe, it's exactly where I needed to be.

Before anyone has the bright idea to take the above passage and slap it on a wooden plank, paint it and sell it, I just ask that I receive 10 percent of the gross profit (we'll also need to negotiate distribution plans and marketing strategies, so please email me with appointment requests). Anyhow, I was talking to El Doc yesterday, and I must admit I wasn't having the best day. My mood wasn't the greatest, so I ended up going off on a tangent about healthcare.

See, there's not another feeling in this world (or at least not one I've experienced, and I've experienced a lot) quite like the one you get, hearing someone tell you that you are too much of a risk/liability for them to help you, even though there's nothing about it that is your fault. I wish I could say that I was as T.A.N. as He-Man afterwards but that would be a lie. I holed up for a good five to ten minutes in my bathroom.

As I was telling this story to El Doc, it was fairly obvious I was passionate about the subject. I guess I've been raised around people who actually care about others. We may have a unique way of expressing this at times, but don't tell us how to help each other; we don't tell you how to be an asshole. When Stubby lost his hand (unfortunately we never found it) I can recall the entire community coming to help during harvest. That's a big deal, city folk. I can't seem to recall a time growing up when one of our own was in trouble and help wasn't soon behind.

This mania has brought people into my life who are simply irreplaceable, while at the same time it has done the impossible and driven people who were once so close to me away. At times I'll hole (simply spin into a black hole within my mind) and dwell on what I've lost during these times, but I can usually pull myself out. I try to be strong and appreciate all that I have in this world, because deep down I know there are a lot of people out there who are struggling more than I can imagine. But at these times I, like so many others, ask myself, what's my calling? My purpose? Why did all of this happen to me, and what am I supposed to do with it?

I think the answer may have come from Cuzin Art:

"There is something speaking through you. Once you learn how to harness it, you're going to be unstoppable."

And El Doc:

"You should be an advocate; they could use you and your skills."

I am obsessed with the Revolutionary War era, with its secrecy, "treason," and new ideas on life. I am particularly fascinated by the Founding Fathers, who stood up and gave a voice to others who simply couldn't or wouldn't. They risked all that they knew to make a change for the better of all. How amazing would it be if I could mimic this in some little way with BMD? To give a voice to those who are unable or unwilling? There are so many things I see as wrong with the treatment of this diagnosis, like calling it an illness to begin with; I do not feel inferior, weak or sick, and that's unfortunately what those words imply within our culture to me. There is so much I want to do, to help and effect change. It's almost too much to believe at this point for me. But then I remember where I came from, and I know I'd rather try to help too much than do nothing at all.

TBC . . .

SESSION

JP: Many people in depression can list fatigue, feelings of worthlessness, difficulty sleeping, poor concentration, as well as many other symptoms that can be difficult to deal with. Were you struggling with some of these when you wrote this entry?

DT: The fatigue and worthlessness did come into play, but I struggled mostly with living too much in the past. During depression, I seem to run to the times in my mind when I wasn't diagnosed yet, and I could see my future as bright and optimistic. When the depression sets in, the light at the end of the tunnel can get pretty dim for me, so I tend to look backwards to what I perceive as better times.

KEY TERMS: STALE PEEPS, BEING CRAZY, UNKNOWN, JUMP
Submitted on 4/13/10
Indigo

My Easter basket was always a little out of the ordinary, although I'm not quite sure what an ordinary Easter basket is. I love stale peeps, so I'd open the package and wait a couple of days to eat them. I still do this. I never really liked milk chocolate bunnies but would crush some white chocolate ones. I've never really been a fan of Cadbury Eggs, peanut butter anything, and jelly beans, which meant I had a lot of cheesy fake green grass in my basket. Despite these quirks of mine, I always looked forward to the Easter basket. When I moved away from home after undergrad, it was always the out of the ordinary things that I missed the most.

This past Easter, I stopped by Monkey's place before heading over to see the family as usual. After several attempts to enter his front door, all foiled by Max's relentless jumping (he's a puppy that's like three years old, do the math) I made it inside. Monkey asked me something that I hadn't really thought about until that point:

"Are you going to be able to do this? Ya know, Chicago and all with being crazy."

Although some may say his approach to the subject could use some work, I wouldn't have it any other way. He did bring up a valid point. I hadn't thought about moving in relation to BMD until this point. I was excited to start a new chapter in my life and ready to put the past behind me. I looked at this as an opportunity to start a new life and never thought of the consequences if I went manic. I only had one response to him:

"I don't know. But we're about to find out."

I have no idea what is going to happen in the next four days, let alone in the next four months, other than knowing I'll make a fool out of myself at multiple points. I have been having some rough times the past couple of months for reasons that are beyond my comprehension. I've never been known as a pessimist or ever really down for any reason for any extended period of time. I've tried to attack each day with a positive outlook and a sense of happiness. No matter what happens, I'm determined not to let my mood be affected by irrelevant circumstances that surround me. But BMD has started to change me a little and I don't like it.

There seems to come times in my life when the unknown and uncertainty become the inevitable, when the right answer isn't clear but a decision must be made. I am more than a little scared that my attempt at a new life will fail. That I'll go manic again, or that my company will find out about my diagnosis and either terminate me or refuse to offer me a position. I'm uneasy about waking up one day and being completely lost once again with nowhere to go but to crawl back home. But I feel like everyone has points in their life in which similar questions (albeit probably not psychosis-related questions) play out, and a decision has to be made. What are you going to do?

I'm going to jump, and see what happens.

SESSION

JP: Chi-Town, The Windy City, Second City, Chicagoland, The Queen of the West, The Garden City. Oh, Chicago is one of my favorite cities, and coincidentally one of my favorite movies as well.

DT: Big shocker there, a musical is one of your favorites.

JP: Well, that and I also heart Catherine Zeta Jones, especially since she recently came out about being bipolar type II.

DT: I knew she had to be crazy to be with Michael Douglas. What, too soon?

KEY TERMS: CHOCOLATE MILK, PATIENCE, ASSSESSMENTS, BEAMER
Submitted on 7/13/10
Indigo

I get my usual, three double cheeses with everything, a bag of Mumfords, and a Mountain Dew. I have been coming to this burger shop to help fight hangovers for a while now, and I suppose I'm a creature of habit. As I wait for my food, a biker and his girlfriend sit beside me, and I nod politely. I'm not sure they even notice me; I'm obviously from out of town. As my burgers are delivered, an old farmer sits beside me, and the waitress gets him his usual of burgers and chocolate milk. He must be a creature of habit as well. I sit there and finish my lunch (which I guarantee will take at least three days off my life; worth it) and take in the conversations around me. I'm just in the middle of it all.

My apologies as it's been awhile since my last post, but another state-to-state move is really a pain in the ass. Since I have moved back from the City of Wind, I haven't really been myself. Not that I exactly know who myself is anymore, but I guess I haven't been what I think I should be. After episode uno, it took me six months to even begin to feel better, so I know I'm not that far off, but I'm not the same either. Not that that's a bad thing. I'm sure a few people are glad I'm not quite myself right now. I wouldn't say that I'm disappointed, ashamed, or down about moving home, but I'm not exactly excited, energetic, or thrilled about it; right in the middle, I suppose.

It does get frustrating, almost as much as watching Shayne Graham attempt to kick clutch field goals, realizing that I'm basically right back where I started two years ago, except I've added another college loan to the mix. But I have to learn to accept it. There are certain things in life that are simply out of my control, and the longer I complain about them, the further I'll get from solving them. I've been scrambling for the past couple of weeks, trying to find a job and not having much success. The two-year hole in my resume could have something to do with that. I suppose I'm worried that the only thing I'll be able to do with my life is work at a store in the mall or something, not that the mall is awful, but it was never part of my career ambitions. I have zero patience when it comes to this because I feel the longer I wait, the smaller the opportunity becomes for me to get my life back on track.

I'm not 100 percent sure that the above is a completely accurate assumption, but it feels real enough for me that panic will set in from time to time. Yesterday I took a big step forward by slowing down and actually trying to set up appointments for my health. Unfortunately, my file was closed, and I'll more than likely have to go through assessments again. I wonder where they'll put me this time, hopefully not in rehab again because I'm not sure how you rehab from BMD. At any rate, I know I need the help, but I know how much of a process it is to get it.

I then woke up this morning after another crazy dream. At least this time I wasn't manic: I was a pitcher for the Reds. I got up from my parents' spare bed, took a call from BMW Financial in concerns of my lease being up and of returning my Big Body Beamer, shaved, showered, and started writing. This really doesn't sound like a big accomplishment, but as I was showering, I recalled it took me at least four months to get to this point after episode uno. I may not be on top of the world right now, but I'm not underneath it either. I'd say I'm right in the middle, working my way up, and even though I know it's going to be a long, tough road, it's better than being on my way down.

SESSION

JP: Dealing with depression can become a full-time job that requires constant adjustments. To help combat these changes, someone with bipolar disorder can be aware not only of their moods but some other key signs of depression, like irritability, sleep problems, inability to experience happiness, and feelings of worthlessness.

DT: Yeah. I also like to try and focus on what I do have in my life and appreciate all of those things that I used to take for granted, like family and friends, in these times of depression.

KEY TERMS: THE MALL, PUBERTY, RESOLUTION, GOOD/BAD DAYS
Submitted on 8/12/10
Indigo

As I was checking out the automated Proactiv machine at the mall, I came to a realization: I'm going through puberty again. Let me tell you, the first time around was not all that great an experience. My reasons for this realization are as follows:

1. My face is breaking out like I'm fifteen.

2. I haven't had any sort of opposite sex interaction in a while.

3. My voice keeps breaking in and out.

4. My bedroom is across from my parents'.

5. I've been to the mall three times in the past week and I'm going back tonight.

I really wish I had some clever tie-in with these facts and my mania, but I don't. I just feel completely weirded out by this and decided to share it. (BTW: the Proactiv Machine is incredibly weird and legit at the same time.)

This week would have been my final week at my internship in Chicago. While I'm disappointed that I wasn't able to complete it, I don't feel like I missed out on much--well, a few things, but nothing a quick claw game can't fix. I think I would have been pretty good there and even could have made it in the City of Wind if my mania hadn't gotten in the way, but that doesn't really change anything now. I've made my New Year's Resolution (so sue me cuz I'm eight months late, but I get a pass, considering I was locked up in Southside! during NYE) and that's to look more to the future than the past.

I've been pretty hard on myself lately and worrying so much about what happened, rather than being optimistic about what might be coming. I know I'm going to have my good and bad days, but lately I've been letting my bad days run over and take over the good. It's almost like lately, I've been getting down on myself for giving too much of a shit.

To combat this, I've decided to take the rest of the year off and focus on getting some sort of healthcare (probably should have done that earlier . . . my blunder), finding a doc (and trying not to be a dick to them) and figuring out my next move. These should be a few, fairly simple tasks to complete, as any normal person would agree, but for some reason I seem to have a lot of problems with them.

Just a final thought on my puberty experiences of late: I wanted to bring up that if any female asks for my number tonight at the mall, I will give it to you. That kind of sounds creepy (probably because it kind of is). See, my first go-around with puberty, I was at the mall (of course) and a girl asked for my number. I immediately said I didn't have a phone (terrible lie) and it wasn't because she wasn't attractive. Mainly, I was so shocked by a girl noticing me that my first reaction was to lie. I still regret this, and don't quite understand it to this day.

SESSION

DT: I'd definitely say this was one of my bad days.

JP: All people suffering from bipolar disorder do have their good and bad days with their ups and downs. However, if these begin to interfere with their ability to work, relate to others and function effectively, it is advisable to seek out a psychiatrist.

DT: Or if you don't feel comfortable seeking out a psychiatrist, as I know they can be a pain in the ass at times--

JP: Not all of us!

DT: Yeah, *all* of ya can be. But seriously, calling someone you trust in your support system and just letting them know what's going on will pay off in the long run. Trust me; I'm not a doctor.

<u>KEY TERMS:</u> SHAME SPIRALS, MR. FEBRUARY, BONDI BEACH, LUCKY
Submitted on 2/11/11
Indigo

Happy Early Valentine's Day Ladies!

Name: Derek Thompson
Wearing: Burberry Trunks ($225)
Also Known As: "That Guy"
Can Be Found: Disregarding His Life

This was my spread for "The Seven Wonders of the World 2004 Calendar" from my study-abroad experience. I was Mr. February and I left my number on Valentine's Day in the calendar, but no one ever called. I pulled this beauty out of storage the other day after watching a little bit of the Travel Channel's "10 Sexiest Beaches." Surprisingly, Enon Beach didn't make the cut.

See, what my depression enjoys doing to me is to basically trap my mind on what I don't have in my life right now. Dwelling over the "what ifs" in my life and then taking me to those places in my mind where they still exist as real. It's a little difficult to explain, but the bottom line is that it sucks and I would like to move on. I can usually pull myself out of these downward shame spirals within a few minutes, but the Big D has been laying it on pretty thick lately.

So the other night, I was flipping channels, trying to forget I was losing $50 on the damn Missouri/Kansas game, when I spotted the "10 Sexiest Beaches" show. I immediately stopped because I've been having a pretty rough year so far and thought some bikinis couldn't hurt the situation; and I was right. Well, come to find out that number six on the list was Bondi Beach in Sydney, Australia. What a coincidence, that's the beach I lived on! No wonder it's number six and not seven on the list. You're welcome, Australia.

I was able to live in one of the "sexiest" places in the world for six months and go to the beach every day. Literally, that's all I did. I ask you, if you had the option of riding two buses (with a connection) for forty-five minutes to sit in a lecture hall for an hour, then have to hop those same bus routes back, *or* sit on a beach in Sydney with topless Aussie women surrounding you, which would you do?

I've been able to experience things in my life I never imagined while growing up in South Chuck. I'm pretty damn lucky and need to start appreciating that and get out of this funk. It's starting to get annoying.

Oh, and one last quick thing: to put all the rumors to rest, yes, there have been discussions about the Seven Wonders of the World considering a comeback calendar (I really, really need to hit the gym).

SESSION

DT: What, no questions or insights into this one, JP?

DT: JP? . . .

DT: JP!

JP: Yeah, depression can be a bitch.

DT: Give me that calendar, you horn dog. Where the hell did you even find that?

JP: So tell me more about Mr. September?

DT: Well, you guys would be perfect for each other, except for the fact that he's not into creepy old men.

JP: Hater in the session; hate, hate, hate, hate.

KEY TERMS: MORSE CODE, BIPOLAR "EXPERT," EXERCISE, GERIATRIC DONG
Submitted on 2/18/11
Indigo

I was at the gym yesterday, and other than creepily staring at the slamming hot body trainer's legs from afar, I was actually working out. I hadn't been to the gym for a while, so I forgot about locker room etiquette. I was bending down, untying my shoes after my workout. I came up slowly and suddenly froze. I was staring down the shaft of an old man's penis; it was as bad as it sounds. I wanted to look away, but the steaming pile of geriatric dong was memorizing. I wondered just how many stories it had and the places it had been. Then it winked at me, I shit you not. The hole opened and shut plain as day. Then it did it again, open and shut. Then a long open count and shut. Winking a few more times and then finally shutting. I heard a grumpy old voice bellow:

"It's Morse code for 'stop staring at my dick'!"

Those old guys know all the tricks.

OK, OK, that didn't really happen, but I will say enough of the story is true that you should still feel sorry for me. I have been working out more, and it's not only because of the slamming hot body trainer. The docs suggest working out and staying as active as possible to help with the mania, depression and everything else in between. It's always toughest for me to do during the winter, though, probably one reason I've been feeling down lately. Not only does it help with the BMD, but I definitely need to get in shape for the upcoming soccer season.

I'm playing on a team this spring with some peeps from high school, so it should be a blast. I really need to get into shape because the last time I played organized soccer, I fell on my face about three times and came home with the best shiner I've ever had (literally ate the ball, what can I say, I'm an athlete). I think it's the little things, like working out and playing some soccer with old friends that I need to break me out of this funk.

I'll admit it, I'm not good at handling bouts of depression. The mania with the craziness of psychosis is a piece of cake compared to the way depression crushes my world around me and suffocates me. Maybe it's because I've had mania my entire life and never really understood what it was inside. I mean, how do you compare those feelings, thoughts and emotions to other kids when no one in the world really understands them? (Which reminds me, how can anyone be an "expert" in bipolar disorder when no one in the world really knows what the hell it is?) I'm not sure of the exact reason, but I do know depression is a bitch.

In case anyone was wondering, after only a few minutes of consideration, I've decided that I am going to ask out the slamming hot body trainer, but I know I have to be creative and unique. I'm sure she's approached constantly by guys wearing baseball caps when they work out and shooting up in the locker room, so I have to make a lasting impression. This is going to be difficult because I don't even know her name, but I do love a challenge. First things first, though. I gotta learn Morse code.

SESSION

JP: Exercise is a great form of release that can have huge benefits for dealing with bipolar disorder. Some other things that seem to work are getting a consistent eight hours of sleep a night, avoiding triggers and stress, and asking for help or not being scared to tell your support system when to back off. Do you have any other tips that work for you?

DT: Find a passion and use it however you can to vent, whatever and however; just something that's truly yours.

JP: Very good suggestion, but I have to jump off subject, to know if you ever saw the old man again after the Morse code incident?

DT: Couldn't tell ya, I keep my eyes down in the locker room now.

BLUE

(DEPRESSED MILD MOODS,
WITHOUT SIGNIFICANT IMPAIRMENT,
ABLE TO WORK)

KEY TERMS: BUCKEYES, SHAME, LISTS, FEELINGS OF FAILURE
Submitted on 10/28/09
Blue

Exhibit A
Phone . . . check.
Wallet . . . check.
Keys . . . check.
Toothbrush . . . cheque.
iPod . . . check.
Shoes . . . chequear.
Belt . . . check.
Shame . . . check. (Don't remember bringing that one with me.)

I've debated with myself (and yes, sometimes aloud to spook my neighbors) on whether or not I should write about my latest mania experience. It doesn't have the thrill of my past experiences and is actually a little boring. OK, OK, if you want me to be completely honest, I wasn't so proud of it and wasn't sure if I wanted to share it. Then I recalled I repeated kindergarten for my inability to share, so I reconsidered. In honor of the cardboard Stop/Go sign hanging from my kindergarten bathroom door, let's flip this thing over and go.

As part of my hobbies, I like to list whenever I am asked to fill out a survey that I enjoy making lists. The reason I enjoy making lists so much is that it is almost impossible to screw up. I mean, it's *your* list. There's not a rule book or right or wrong way. Try it right now and list your Top 5 favorite holiday candies:

1.)   Stale Peeps (Easter)

2.)   White Chocolate Easter Bunny (Easter)

3.)   Multi-color Candy Canes (X-Mas)

4.)   Nerds (Halloween)

5.)   Buckeyes (Whenever I can get them)

See my point? It's almost impossible to mess this up. However, from the evidence provided in Exhibit A, I seem to have managed to achieve the impossible.

This past weekend, I departed from The Nasty to make my way to C-Bus for a celebration of all celebrations, a wedding. As before any trip, I made a list and packed my things for the haul up north. I brought everything I needed and completed my travel list without any hang-ups or mistakes. But on my departure list, things got a little dicey. I ended up bringing back some shame that I know I didn't come up with, and I figured out where it came from.

BMD will throw me a curveball every once in a while, just to make sure I'm still on my toes. As much as I enjoy the random emotional twists it graciously lets me encounter, they can be a bit annoying. I've struggled with a range of emotions while learning to handle BMD that have had me in denial, confusion, acceptance, and hatred with everything else in between; so I thought I had seen them all ("Not so fast, my friend," Corso, College Gameday 2009).

For reasons that I am for some reason embarrassed about, I became very ashamed of myself over this past weekend. I was seeing old friends and seeing how they were taking the next step in their lives. Getting married, buying a house, moving to a new city, starting a family, and having their careers take off. I began to envy all of these things. I stepped back and looked at where I was. A twenty-eight-year-old single guy, starting over from scratch because I had failed.

Not once prior to this had I ever felt like a failure. Not when I was committed, not when I called Porter Hospital's psych ward home for a week, not when I had to move home, not when I had to resign from my job, never until then. It was a lot to take at first, and I struggled with it, but a crazy thing happened (pun intended): I understood it. I don't think I would like being the kind of person who doesn't self-criticize and doesn't feel the consequences of failure. While I know what happened was not my fault, that doesn't mean I should write it off and not learn from it. Maybe I ignored the shameful feelings for a while because I wasn't strong enough at the time to handle them. But now I know what they are and where they come from, and it motivates me to not go back. So although my list wasn't the same as when I left The Nasty, it's more complete now.

SESSION

JP: Shame--

DT: Shameless plug time: go to www.dbsalliance.org and make a donation. It will make you feel better about that sin you recently committed.

JP: Wait, wait, www.dbsalliance.org, correct?

DT: Yeah, but you're going to have to make a lot more than one donation for the sins you've been up to, mister.

JP: Erroneous!

KEY TERMS: SPRING BREAK, PATIENCE, RECOVERY TIME, CITY OF WIND
Submitted on 3/9/10
Blue

<u>March 1, 2010 at 10:10 AM</u>

I'm 30,000 feet in the air right now and I'm not manic, which is different to say the least. I'm somewhere over Ohio on the way to the Pennsylvania state line, and the sun is shining. I'm listening to my music and "Hey There Delilah" is playing and Denver is on my mind. I'm supposed to be heading to Chi-Town to internship-hunt, but I needed a break. I'm reading *Electroboy: A Memoir of Mania* and feeling some relief that someone else may understand the craziness in my life. I'm feeling a bit guilty for actually taking a vacation, considering that for the past two years, I've only worked four months. I'm dwelling on sleeping on the floor at the foot of my mom and stepdad's bed when I was manic. I'm trying to catch the ideas running wild in my mind. I'm confused and looking for answers that will never be found. I'm intimidated by the truth and terrified of the unknown. I'm on vacation . . .

Present Day (March 9, 2010)

I had one of the worst and best vacations I have ever had last week. Since graduating from Wittenberg University almost five years ago (it seems like only yesterday I was streaking the Hollow totally sober and able-minded) I really haven't had a vacation. Whenever I had any extended time off work, I would plan a trip home, where I would likely make some bad decisions. Don't get me wrong, I less than three (<3, get it now?) the ocean and beach like any other winter-trapped Midwesterner, but there's something about home that refuses to let go.

In any case, I was going to use this spring break as an opportunity to take my first vacation since spring break '03 (my first cruise and first time I've been booed off a dance floor). To be honest, I did feel a little bit guilty for taking a trip, due to the fact that all I've done in the past twenty-five months is work about four of them and try to enjoy life the rest. But damn it, also in that time span, I've gone manic and been hospitalized twice for two weeks at a shot, quit two jobs unwillingly, moved back home with my parents, battled depression, visited numerous doctors, resisted being put into outpatient rehab, and been a test subject, and I WANTED A BREAK! (I'm sorry for yelling.)

I had always wanted to visit Costa Rica from the stories Stubby told us but never could find the time while working, so I decided to give my internship hunt a break. I wasn't getting much feedback from the agencies, and the lone piece feedback I received wasn't favorable (politic way of saying it sucked ass). I decided a week before spring break I'd cancel my trip to Chi-Town for internship hunting and take a trip to deserted beaches, lush tropical vegetation, pristine clear waters, and hopefully away from my manic mind back home. The only problem was there would be three of us on this trip: I was the third wheel with my old man and his lady . . . what had my life come to? There was not enough time to get her a passport, so we swapped Costa Rica with Key West, an even swap if you ask me.

Not really an even swap at all to come and find out after this trip. Now I've never been a big fan of motorcycles but I understood the appeal (I officially rescind this). Please recall I had my mind set on getting away and clocking out for a week. You can imagine the difficulty with this when it's bike week in Florida. I love walking down the street at dusk, just enjoying the views and the atmosphere of the Keys. I was doing this when six middle-aged accountants from Cleveland rode by on their Harleys. And were kind enough to let me know how just how T.A.N. they think they were by revving their bikes at me; thanks boys, I really appreciated it. The remote beaches and warm ocean were swapped out for near-record lows in temperatures and 30 MPH gusts of wind. I got had.

I had a couple of very bad days in Key West, and they were the type of days that kind of made me want to change something. But I kept forgetting I'd only been out of the hospital for two months, and the last time I had an episode, I was packing my things and moving home from Denver and battling the first stage of depression at two months out from the ward. I spread myself thin at times, trying to prove something to myself. This has yet to work to my benefit, and yesterday I had to quit my volunteer-position with (Radio Edit). It wasn't something I wanted to do because I did really enjoy hanging out with the kids, but it had to be done.

On a brighter note, I was selected for an interview with the sports marketing agency in Chicago I've been wanting all along. I go this Friday and then get to stay in the City of Wind for the St. Patty's Day Parade: I'll be this guy. . .

(Yeah that shirt reads: Me + Green Beer = Your St. Patty's Day Mistake)

I also get to hang out with my sister again (BTW, we got dead last in the flip cup tourney . . . no finger-pointing, but a certain pony wasn't on point). Look out, Chicago, this guy might be on his way . . . Go Sox! (I refuse to root for the Chubs.)

SESSION

JP: Well, Derek, it seems as though you struggled with the extended recovery time associated with your manic episode here. This is common; you know, some people may be able to recover quickly from a manic, hypomanic, mixed or depressive episode, but for many others, it is more gradual. Often, it takes a few months for a person's functioning to return to familiar levels. This may be true even if symptoms of the most recent episode have been fully eliminated. The time needed to recover often frustrates people with bipolar disorder. Healthcare providers often need to clarify the recovery phase for patients, their families and employers.

A person recovering from a broken leg would increase activities gradually. Similarly, gradually increasing activities after a bipolar episode is advised. This approach allows people to take on responsibilities and build self-confidence more manageably. Some individuals rush back into full, if not increased, activities. They may be trying to convince themselves and others that they are fully recovered. This "flight into health" often exhausts and defeats people. Many individuals who expect a lot of themselves are unhappy with how slowly they recover. They feel demoralized by the delay. This seems to hit home from this entry.

DT: Yeah, it's definitely something I've struggled with. Patience doesn't really run in the family. NEXT ENTRY!

KEY TERMS: DRUG DEALS, CHILD PLEASE, PRICKS, FANTASY FOOTBALL
Submitted on 8/4/10
Blue

The start of football season is just around the corner, which means I'm getting peer-pressured to join Fantasy Football Leagues (dibs on team name "Cap'n Geech and the Shrimp Shack Shooters"), planning road trips (Oct 22 A-Town for the Dirty Birds vs. the Who Deys!?, in the eloquent words of Ocho-Cinco "Child please!") and checking out the lines for the up-coming year. Last year, I was only three games away from pulling in six grand and hijacking a plane to Awesomeville, so this year I feel like I have some expectations to live up to. As always I'll take a look at the over under for the Bengals (eight, if I was a betting man I'd take the over; and I am so I will), odds at winning the Super Bowl (off the board right now, thanks a ton, Brett) and I've added one this year, and that is the over under of number of phone calls I'll make before being able to get a doctor's appointment.

Finding a doctor who will see you without insurance is about as likely as Pittsburgh Steelers fans from Ohio acting like they're not conceited pricks. When I left the hospital in The Nasty (Southside!) I was first a participant in a study being conducted through the hospital and UC, so I was "lucky enough" to see a doctor once a week for ten weeks. I suppose I should be grateful for the help I received while in the study, but it just became annoying.

Every week I had the opportunity to be a learning tool for a new assistant still getting the hang of taking blood. Then I was able to describe my emotions and feelings and mania to some-one who really can't understand it. It seems to me that being in a manic episode and then trying to describe this to someone who hasn't had one would compare to trying to describe a sunset to someone who can't see it; it's just something you need to experience. At least I was seeing a doc and having my prescription wrote (written? wrought? whatever).

Once I left the study, I was aligned with an organization that was a sort of middleman to get me in contact with the guys with the good meds. This is starting to sound like a drug deal, probably because it was. My first assessment determined that I was an addict, and they attempted to put me in outpatient rehab (no, thank you) where my behavior relating to addiction would be emphasized and mental health put to the side. This, of course, would have been great if I was addicted to anything other than being sweet and I wasn't diagnosed with bipolar disorder and suffering from chronic psychotic episodes (but I'm sure Bud Light is my problem).

So next I was referred to a service that concentrated on addressing my mental condition and issues, but alas, I didn't have a Medicare/'Caid/'whoknows card. I had never conducted my phone interview, of which I was never called by said agency so could not conduct my interview but naturally that was my fault. The service couldn't accept me. After sliding my doc a few extra bones (I kid I kid) he wrote me a prescription, and I took off for the City of Wind (mistake).

Well, after three phone calls, two denials, one unreturned message and a near-episode, I decided to move back to Ohio (there were a few other stories in there that I'll share when I'm more comfortable with this relationship). So now I'm back in Clark County and back to my search for help. To be fair, since I've returned last week, I've made five phone calls and I'm still without an appointment, so I'm going to put the over under at nine. I believe this is line will attract betters on both sides and provide a little change in my pocket. There's plenty of room, it's not like I have my medicine in there or anything.

SESSION

JP: I'm assuming you were having issues with insurance due to your preexisting condition of bipolar disorder. In case anyone doesn't know, insurance agencies define a preexisting condition as a health condition that existed prior to someone applying for a health insurance policy or enrolling in a new plan. Insurance companies and health plans are concerned about their financial bottom line--it's in their best interest, therefore, to exclude people with a preexisting condition, impose a waiting period before coverage starts, or charge higher premiums and out-of-pocket expenses. Given this, and with your past experiences discussed in the entry, what are your thoughts on the subject, Derek?

DT: I call bullshit.

KEY TERMS: CONFIDENCE, ONLINE DATING, CREATIVITY, POLAR BEARS
Submitted on 8/19/10
Blue

How much does a polar bear weigh?

Enough to break the ice. Hi, I'm Derek.

Now what women could resist that charm and humor? Well, apparently at least three from The Nasty via Match.com. I couldn't believe it either.

A peculiar new thing my mania has decided to start playing with is my self-confidence. I've never really had a problem with this before. Some may say I'm a bit dickish, but jealousy will get you nowhere my friends. I was usually pretty confident in the person I was. I had everything planned out in my head on how my life would take shape and felt confident about making it happen.

I'm sure just about everyone does this planning whether they intend to or not; human nature, I suppose. The farm gene that seems to be in all my relatives just kind of skipped me for some reason, probably to make room for the BMD gene; what are the odds? Growing up, I knew that in order to make it, I was going to have to educate myself. So that's what I did, and I liked it so much I repeated kindergarten and my senior collegiate year and once I finally appeared to be graduating, I took the next step and got a job. I was working hard and finding success and could see my life plan coming together.

This of course came to a screeching halt--figuratively and literally as I tried to drive my Big Body Beamer off the top of a parking garage during episode uno. I saw everything I had worked for disappear, and with it went my confidence. Coming to terms with my psychotic manic episodes, filled with hallu-cinations and delusions, actually came pretty easily to me; so weird, I know. Yet regaining my self-confidence is something I struggle with on a nearly daily basis.

In order to counter this, I decided to give myself a little pick-me-up. You know, go after the ole sure thing to boost the ole self-esteem and get yourself back on track. When I had to resign from my internship in the City of Wind and knew I would have to move back home and start over again, I needed a boost. I needed a fun activity to boost my confidence and entertain myself for the next month until I moved. Of course, I immediately thought of online dating.

That whole eHarmony "system" looked way too complicated for me, so I hopped on board for one month of service at Match. com. My idea was to write about my online dating experiences and provide even further entertainment for my readers (I'm that dedicated to you all). I also felt this would be the self-confidence booster I needed to pick me up after falling on my face again in the City of Wind. I mean, how hard can it be to get some action via online dating, right?

Wrong. I once again amazed myself at how bad I must be at this whole dating thing, considering I got zero, I repeat zero, responses from my polar bear line. I will admit rejection online is a lot easier to deal with, though.

SESSION

JP: Maintaining self-confidence while living with bipolar disorder can become what at times seems like an uphill battle. But if you think that bipolar disorder is simply a "disorder one has," then you're wrong. It's a symptom of very high creativity and energy levels which are found in most geniuses. Does that help with your self-confidence?

DT: Yeah, actually, it does. Thanks, JP; that was really helpful.

JP: You're very welcome. I'm just not sure if there is a lick of credibility to it as I just found it online at http://www.bipolar-disorder-uncovered.com.

DT: Whatever, I like it. Besides, when has a random website on the World Wide Web ever not been credible?

KEY TERMS: <u>RESIGNATION</u>, AT&TIZZLE LIFER, (RADIO EDIT), NEW DOCS
Submitted on 11/5/10
Blue

Letter of Resignation (Health Reasons)

Hello (Radio Edit),
I wanted to begin this letter by thanking you and (Radio Edit) for this opportunity that I was looking forward to. However, the past three years, I have been battling a health issue that I was confident we had under control. Unfortunately, symptoms reappeared during training yesterday, and after discussions with my doctors, they have advised me to take the treatment in another direction. This change in treatment will require me to resign effective immediately to concentrate on my health. My apologies for this as no one is more disappointed than me, but my health must take priority over my career at this point.

 Thank you once again for your time.
Good luck in the future,
Derek L. Thompson

Unfortunately, I am becoming quite comfortable (and quite good, I might add) at writing letters of resignation like the above. When I started at AT&Tizzle, I can recall one of my apprentices (scarily, they gave me three to train) remarking that I would be an AT&T lifer. I didn't object to it the least bit. I enjoyed my job and the people I worked with, so I didn't see any immediate reason to leave. A psychotic manic episode changes that, and two of them change everything. I guess the point I'm driving at is that I never imagined myself quitting a job after college. Now I've quit four in the past three years.

 What's new about this last resignation is that while I'm disappointed it didn't work out, I'm not the least bit frustrated with it. Following the previous three resignations, I was so upset and frustrated afterwards that it took me a month to get my head straight. This time it took me the drive from Nashville to Louisville, not too shabby. I think there are two reasons for this change: the fact that I saw it coming, and my new docs (amazing, I know).

This past week, my first day of training at my new job went really well and I enjoyed myself. That night, I lay down and nothing went through my mind--well, about a few thoughts at a time, but that's really nothing for me. I was able to focus without much work, and my mind was at what seemed like peace. I wasn't tensed up at all. I was completely relaxed with a calm sensation engulfing me; it was great. For the first time in a couple of years, I didn't feel like I was wound a little tight, and my mind wasn't chasing ideas from here to there and back. I felt at peace . . . Something was wrong with how good I felt.

I was right. An hour and a half into my next day of training, my head began to hurt and I felt nauseous. I stepped outside to get some air and it hit me: I spent the next couple of hours fighting off my mania. It came at me in waves, sending me up and down and bringing me to my knees until I gave up and quit and drive home. I'm just glad I saw it coming and caught it, with having to quit my job being the only consequence. Two trips to the wards is my limit.

TBC . . .

SESSION

JP: Finding a job with bipolar disorder can be very challenging, sometimes a seemingly impossible task. I do not have much work in this area, so I went online and found some helpful tips from Madeleine Kelly, who wrote *Bipolar and the Art of Roller-coaster Riding*:

- A bipolar-resistant job is one that is protected from discrimination and unfair dismissal. Some jobs are more bipolar-resistant than others; for example, seasonal rural jobs and permanent jobs where there is cumulative sick leave.

- You can do a lot to improve your job's security against discrimination.

- Don't tell your secret. If you have not disclosed to anyone at work that you have bipolar, keep it that way.

- Do as much as you can to stay well. Find out about the large number of steps you can take.

- Protect your reputation. If you doubt that you can get through a day without symptoms messing things up, stay at home, even if it means a day without pay. To go to work could mean you lose your job.

- If you have told your boss, ask for workplace changes that will make a difference to your health; for example, starting a bit later so any sedative side effects have worn off.

- Use your allies. Confide in a trustworthy friend. Tell your friend some of the signs of oncoming illness and ask him or her to let you know if they see them. That way, you have not only yourself watching for symptoms, but also an objective friend. Then you can take action to prevent the illness from getting worse.

- If you end up losing another job because of bipolar, look at it as an opportunity to do something better, more prosperous, or more interesting. Each time you dust yourself off you add to your knowledge, stamina and wisdom.

What do you think?

DT: Well, I think that if that kind of writing can get published, I shouldn't have any trouble with this book. You really phoned that one in, didn't ya, JP?

JP: I have a migraine, I'm nauseous, I feel like hell and--

DT: Look like shit.

JP: For your information, I have the flu, and with that compassion it's no wonder you're still single.

KEY TERMS: SHOOTING STARS, HOT TUBS, SMALL GIFTS, APPRECIATION
Submitted on 11/12/10
Blue

"As much hell as it's been the past three years, and I know it's been hell, Derek, bipolar disorder does have its gifts. They may be small but they are there."
—New counselor who I don't hate so much

I forgot how much I love the country night sky. The past week, I took a couple of nights to wander out into the pasture beside the house to get away, looking like a crazy person standing in the middle of a pasture in the middle of nowhere. It's been ten years since I've lived in the country, and I missed how peaceful it can be (and how irritating, Mickey Mouse 3--Derek 0).

In high school, I used to spend just about every fall and winter night in our hot tub, dreaming about losing my V-Card and getting lost in the night sky. I suppose some people use meditation, some read, others veg out in front of the boob tube, some drive to nowhere, others watch sunsets to free themselves; but I prefer the cliché 1970s porn set of a hot tub at night under the stars. Just a romantic at heart, I guess.

So of course, with the way things have been going, our hot tub died a couple of weeks ago. To compensate for this, I wandered out to the pasture this week to look up at the night sky and get away. After the coyotes stopped crying and the dogs stopped howling, I found myself surrounded by nothing. It was great.

Earlier in the week:
> It was cool out, but the wind had died down
> from the day and the night breeze was mini-
> mal at best. The air was calm and the world

seemed asleep. I was alone out there, and I wasn't scared of that fact for the first time in a while. I lifted my head and caught a glimpse of a shooting star in the east and literally laughed aloud. I hadn't seen a shooting star in so long, I think I had forgotten they even existed. At about the time I got back to focusing on the country star- speckled sky, another shooting star came from the west. I know I had to look like a crazy person because now I started laughing aloud to myself and prancing about.

The next time I went out, I saw two more shooting stars in the sky, and it made me glad I spit out those pills three years ago.

My new counselor and I have been working on a new approach to fighting this BMD. Focusing on the little gifts it provides that seem so insignificant at first; just like the falling rocks in space that seemingly have no purpose or reason to exist except to fall through space, until they hit Earth's atmosphere and begin to heat up and burn. Glowing hotter and hotter, one by one they light up the country night sky, giving me a show unlike any I could see in any theater, cinema, or venue.

So I guess that's the reason I haven't let quitting my job bother me. I'm starting to see the little gifts in my life more and more. I just wish they included my hot tub.

SESSION

JP: I think your counselor hits it right on the head with his gifts statement above.

DT: Yep, me too, that's why I don't hate him so much.

KEY TERMS: BELIEVE
Submitted on 2/7/11
Blue

BELIEVE

I'd like to welcome my readers to my manic experience
Where my doc insists that in order to survive I've got to
find new ways to fight
So I get down on my knees, look up to the sky and
ask God why
Why did he put this evil pain so deep down inside
Was I not a good servant, were my sins too lustful in
nature to hide
Just then it hits me, it's my mania to blame for this game
Which means I've got vengeance on my mind and
something to say
I may be crazy but that grain still runs through these veins
Which is just my complicated way to say that I'm a country
boy to the core
And that's just something that you ain't never gonna change
So when you had me defeated and asking not to wake
when I pray
My family swooped in and saved the day
Reached down into my darkness and pulled me up out
of my grave
So I could spit out those pills to live to fight another day
Oh and remember how you took that girl that I once
hated with all my might
And then shifted her into that girl that I'd protect with
all my life
Taking something so simple as an insignificant paper clip
And having it trigger me further down into my
psychotic manic trip
Where my dreams become reality as I get lost in my
own singularity
While you plant the seed of divinity deep within the
essence of me
Of a chosen one who was sent here to make all believe

Only to wake up cold, crying, and alone on the psych
ward's bathroom floor
But I've picked myself up and I'm here with no fear
asking you for more
Finally standing on my own two legs, looking dead into
your sight
And letting you know that I'm the one here who's looking
for a fight
Oh and that girl you had me chasing through my mind
Racing so fast that I thought I stopped time
Well I gave her the most important thing you took from me
See I gave her the choice on how involved she wants to be
In this insanity that they call you and me
And now suddenly it's all clear to me
I'm becoming the man I was always undoubtedly destined
to be
Standing before thee on my day of judgment
With Christopher on my left and the Good Witch Glinda
on my right
I've made peace with the Man upstairs so you know whose
back He's got in this fight
We'll see how you like living within the shadows of the
darkness of your fear and your fright
Because once I possess the light, I'll pass it on to illuminate
the night
And this simply means that I'll take my vengeance once
when we meet in the afterlife
So listen, because the only sound you're bound to hear
Will be my chant in the night as I march towards our fight
Oooooh weeeee Oh-Ooooooooooh Oh!
I'll be marching with a chip on my shoulder and another
one on my knee
I'm the man behind the curtain sent here to make
all believe.

SESSION

JP: This is addressed to your mania, but you have it listed as
a depressed mood. Why is that?

DT: Whenever my depression starts to send me down a hole, I try to use something to fight back. When I wrote this, I was fighting depression and looking for something to pick me up. For whatever reason, it helped to recite this whenever things looked bleak.

JP: So who's the girl?

DT: Well, that's kind of tricky.

JP: See, girls are so difficult, Derek. You should just follow my lead and give them up.

DT: Thanks for the advice, JP, but I'm going to stay on my team. I already have the equipment you guys play with.

KEY TERMS: FOOTLONG BRAT, GAINER, FAMILY, FRIENDSHIP ILLUSIONS

Submitted on 3/4/11

Blue

"DO A GAINER STEVIE! DO A GAINER STEVIE!"

You could hear this chant being screamed at the South Chuck pool while I was growing up. It was my brothers and I standing at the deep end, yelling up at the high dive for our pool hero to do a back somersault and get us drenched from the splash. I had no idea at that point that in a mere fifteen years, I'd be carrying my childhood pool hero up to his honeymoon suite from the hotel pool in Vegas on the day of his wedding, suffering from possible heat stroke, alcohol poisoning, or a little bit of both. Don't worry; we got him a footlong brat for the elevator ride up and made him close his eyes so he wouldn't see the bride before the wedding and ruin everything.

Growing up in a small town could at times feel like just like a family, and Stevie from above was like our older cousin, entertaining us up on that high dive during the summers. I've met friends along the way in college and vagabonding around the country, and unfortunately, I've lost touch with the majority of them. I don't think I'm different from anyone else in regard to seeing friendships kind of drift away naturally. I don't mind this because I know it's inevitable, but losing friendships for reasons that are nearly unexplainable to me is tough.

BMD has undoubtedly put people in my life that I could not replace. The support I've received over the past few years has blurred the line between family and friends. At the same time, it has taken friendships from me that I never thought it possible to lose. I've witnessed friendships dissipate right before my eyes for reasons that I still have trouble comprehending. I have spent countless hours dwelling on people I felt had abandoned me.

At these times, I become infatuated with what I think I have lost, under the illusion that my friends walked away from me in my direst time of need. The truth of the matter is they were never my friends to begin with; they were my drinking buddies (nothing wrong with that, I loved to drink). I always seem to have a difficult time determining the difference between my friends, who are basically family, and my drinking buddies, who are only acquaintances. I suppose I just want to have as big a family as possible which includes my friends, and that just can't be a reality. Some people plain don't care; that's all right, but I really should stop giving a shit about them, too. While BMD hasn't been a picnic, it has taught me some valuable life lessons, and one of those lessons is: there's nothing like good family and friends.

I think I'm starting to come out of depression (finally, you bitch) and beginning to enjoy life a little more. It's harder than it sounds at times; give me a break, I'm bipolar. I had a couple of options to "celebrate" this coming-out party, which included heading back to Vegas or heading down to A-Town to visit some Southern family and friends. My last Vegas trip was a blast (Shay and I saved the wedding, no thanks needed) but Southern belles come first (or not all when they seem to be with me). I haven't seen Rhett (not a Southern name at all, I still heart it though, sis) since he was born, so I'm making a trip down South next week to "celebrate," which means it's going to be off the heezy fo' sheezy you can find me up in One Tweezy.

SESSION

JP: Drinking buddies huh? More like "My Buddy"; look at you and your cute little doll:

DT: Ha-ha-ha, I did love that damn doll. But for the sake of further damages to my reputation and manhood, can I have any other pictures you may have taken from my albums while I was in the bathroom?

NORMAL
(GREEN)

ABSTRACT:

THE NORMAL SECTION OF THE MOOD CHART IS CONSTANT FOR THE ENTIRE SECTION. GREEN WILL BE USED TO REPRESENT ALL THE ENTRIES IN THIS SECTION. THIS MOOD IS CHARACTER- IZED BY NO IMPAIRMENT, WITH THE ABILITY TO WORK THROUGHOUT. THIS SECTION CONSISTS OF TWENTY-SEVEN ENTRIES WITH GREEN REPRESENTING EVERY ENTRY.

GREEN

(NORMAL MOODS WITHOUT
IMPAIRMENT, ABLE TO WORK)

KEY TERMS: LOST, TOMMY TOUGHNUTS, "EVERYTHING," CONFUSED
Submitted on 6/23/09
Green

What a bizarrely unpredictable world we live in.

This was about the only phrase I could come up with while pondering life the other day and trying to describe the everyday events and circumstances I've experienced in the past year and a half or so of my life. At this time of pondering, I was driving back from an interview process when I started to recall where I've been and what's been going on since I "thought" I knew what life was all about. Not eighteen months ago, I had everything figured out. I was on the fast track to success.

As soon as I had graduated from college, I packed up and left the small-town life of Ohio for the big city of A-Town. I had received a great apprenticeship opportunity with an industry-leading telecommunications company, with seemingly endless room for growth. I was on the fast track, making my way to the top, moving all along the way from A-Town to Denver and on to my next stop in San Jose. I thought I was Tommy Toughnuts and I had the whole world figured out, but then I woke up in a psych ward.

To be honest, it really did feel like that, like all of a sudden everything I thought I knew and understood about life and the world was completely gone. Prior to the Denver psych ward, I had been spending the first couple of months in 2008 planning my relocation to San Jose, to start a new position that was essentially a promotion. Sure, I was feeling higher than ever before, but I simply thought that I was excited to be moving and starting a new job in a new city by the beach, like I'd always dreamed of while "cornfield locked" growing up in Ohio. I was in that part of my life when I figured I knew what it took to be successful and happy, and I was just living it.

Less than three months later, I was living at home with my parents, jobless and completely lost. I was unable to take care of myself anymore and didn't know where to turn or what to do next. My life felt like it turned a 180 on itself, and I was completely confused. My episode had started sometime in the middle of

January 2008 and didn't end until the middle of June that same year. During those few months, I thought I had lost "everything." But the crazy thing is that I'm not upset about it. Sure, this time last year, I was devastated, but now I'm happy it happened. I've realized you can't appreciate or know what you truly have until you think you have lost "everything."

SESSION

JP: I'm a little confused by your last statement. What exactly do you mean?

DT: Well, I just meant that what used to matter so much in my life back then might not be what's important to me anymore, and that's a good thing. For instance, I spent so much time invested in my career that it took away from my personal, social and family life.

KEY TERMS: DANCING BEAR, HANGOVER, *UNBREAKABLE*, SELF-ESTEEM
Submitted on 7/2/09
Green

It's 1 a.m. this past Thursday morning (that's Wednesday night for you time-challenged peeps, don't feel bad, I'm in the same boat with ya) and I'm standing beside a guy dressed like a bear, dancing on a bar with a beer in my hand and a buzz in my head. There are so many things that are not right with this situation that I don't really know where to start; the guy dressed like a bear would probably be the best place. I'm looking around and decide it's time to leave. I know I'm going to pay for this tomorrow.

Just three hours prior to the dancing bear incident, I was lying in bed, knowing I wasn't going to do anything that night. It just wasn't worth it the next day. I'm not saying that going out in The Nasty isn't a good time, but I've learned that whenever I venture out, I end up indulging myself in some adult beverages, and they like to play with my mind later. I'm not trying to downplay anyone else's hangover, because I've seen some of my good friends fight the good fight against the alcohol demon the next day and feel nothing but bad for them. However, after I drink, my next day is more than likely filled with rapid mood cycling from BMD, sending me on a whirlwind of a day.

See, I spend a decent amount of my time trying to figure out this BMD I've been handed, and that entails a lot of control battles. I'm sure everyone has had some sort of sports injury throughout their life that lets them sort of relate to this (and if not, you're more than likely the inspiration for Bruce Willis's character in his worst movie ever, *Unbreakable*, and I pity you). With that injury, you always have downtime when you are simply unable to run, walk, write, turn your head, lift something or whatever the case may be. During this downtime, you can lose trust in whatever you've injured and lose belief that you'll ever be the same again.

Eventually, your injury heals, and you are back to your old self before you know it. But there's always some time right after you're cleared by your doctor, when you're timid while you learn to trust whatever you injured again. You know you're OK, but in the back of your mind, you can still faintly recall your pain and distrust. Over time, you begin to forget about the injury as it slides to the back of your mind, and then eventually it's gone and you are back to your old self.

That unfortunately is not going to be a reality for me; I'm always going to have BMD. So I struggle, trying to believe in my mind and trust myself again, and it can get tough. I'm not trying to say that my mind is broken, or that *I'm* broken and can't be fixed; I'm just saying that I'm a little different now and am still learning to handle everything. It's similar to when I used to injure myself in sports and then got healed up and ready to go back. The next time I played the sport in which I'd injured myself, I often started out by going at it from a slightly different angle. Right now, I'm looking for that angle with BMD.

I think for me, one of those new angles may be to go out and have a few drinks with a friend and try to forget everything for a little bit. It's funny how going out on a Wednesday night in The Nasty's downtown with a dancing bear can make me feel a little like my old self, and how good that can feel sometimes. Is it the solution? No, I know that; but to try and use as many sports analogies as possible in this entry, it's like sending a baseball player back down to the minors to find his swing. They should know they aren't going to stay down there for the rest of their career, but it has a purpose, and why not try to enjoy the time that you are down there?

On a non-sport note, I didn't smoke one fag last night, and the one I took from the bathroom attendant, I gave to the homeless guy on my walk home. Which was my good deed for the day, in a weird way.

SESSION

JP: So is your reference to the minor league player an attempt at a comparison to yourself being essentially demoted in your life some way with bipolar disorder?

DT: Absolutely. I was still recovering from my first episode and depending heavily on my family for support to live at the time I wrote this entry.

JP: This reminds me of a study I read a few years back that took a look at 166 patients, all men aged twenty-eight, after their first manic episode. Two years later, roughly 65 percent of them had yet to achieve functional recovery, which is to return to the level of independent living, work, and school status that they had a month before the manic episode.

DT: Yeah, talk about being a real bitch for your self-esteem.

KEY TERMS: CARNIES, KINGS ISLAND, TOTALLY BOSS, CALIFORNIA GAMES
Submitted on 7/14/09
Green

There are a few things that I fear in this world, and one is the spinning carnival rides at the county fair. Another is "Carnies. Circus folk. Nomads, you know. Smell like cabbage. Small hands." You are probably thinking to yourself right now: "Yeah, who doesn't fear Carnies? But what's up with the spinning carnival rides? Those things rock!"

For your information, I fear those rides because I always seem to boot after my turn on them. It's pretty damn embarrassing; well, I guess as embarrassed as one can get on the midway of the Clark County Fair. I came to the realization today that at times I can be just a little kid stuck in a grown-up's body.

I spent most of my day today at one of my favorite childhood hot spots, King's Island. Now, while my day didn't start out the greatest (we had to park in Drop Tower 39, man, whatever happened to Scrappy Doo 12?) the day was nonetheless radical (yeah, that's a term from my childhood, pretty tubular, huh?). I was a bit upset that the Smurfs ride is no longer in existence, but my disappointment soon faded as I concentrated on my model shoot via the roller-coaster's cameras. The double finger point with mouth open on the Diamondback, the double rock out fists with tongue out on the Vortex, the pondering in the opposite direction shot on the Beast, and the always classic double arm flex on the Diamondback; yeah we rode that one a few times as it's wicked cool. I'm not gonna lie, being a kid was totally boss.

For some reason, during my episode last year, I reverted back to my childhood for certain portions of time. I became obsessed with video games again (Guitar Hero dominated my life) and I'm the furthest thing from a gamer you can find, aside from California Games, of course. I would still to this day binge drink on Hi-C Ecto Cooler from the tin can while playing that incredible Nintendo masterpiece all night long. I also stocked my fridge and freezer with all of my favorite childhood foods. My favorite would have to be Eggo Blueberry Waffles. Growing up, my dad used to create these unbelievably good Eggo breakfasts on Saturday mornings as my brothers and I "rotted" our brains on cartoons. Speaking of those cartoons (which I'm still secretly kind of obsessed with) I came out of my episode with a complete file on my computer dedicated to pictures of Foghorn Leghorn . . .

. . . My apologies for that delay. I just spent the last twenty minutes watching Foghorn Leghorn cartoons on the Internet, and they are *still* hilarious.

That's just one of the many bizarre experiences and random past obsessions that resurfaced during my episode. I mean, I hadn't had any desire to play, let alone purchase, any gaming system since I was in middle school, but I bought an Xbox 360 and played the crap out of it during those couple of manic months back in Denver. I hadn't watched a Foghorn Leghorn cartoon since the late 1980s, yet suddenly I couldn't get enough of them. Lastly, my diet--well, when I ate; see, I managed to lose about twenty pounds during the episode. I'm thinking of marketing this diet plan around the tag line: "Drop inches from your waistline, while only partially losing your mind!"

Anyhow, back to my original train of thought: my diet consisted mainly of my childhood favorites. I didn't even know they still sold most of them in stores.

While these may totally seem off the wall (probably because they are) they are a big part of who I am, and I think I forgot about them in the process of growing up and kind of lost who I was. This makes it difficult for me to call BMD a disease or illness when I think it's played a big part in helping me find myself again. Even if that person is a theme- park junky with an addiction to 1950s-era cartoons who yearns for the taste of Ecto Cooler out of the tin can; basically a big kid.

SESSION

JP: I think bipolar disorder is a mental illness where the nerve cells in the brain fail to transmit signals. And although a single cause of bipolar disorder cannot be determined, some chemicals in the brain, particularly neurotransmitters, appear at different levels in patients, compared with those without the disorder. Neurotransmitters are the chemicals responsible for exchanging information about specific functions within the brain, such as memory processing and operating the senses. In patients with bipolar disorder, levels of dopamine, a neurotransmitter that helps manage pleasure, are usually at levels higher than in non-patients during a manic episode, and lower during depressive episodes. This isn't necessarily a confirmation that dopamine is the cause, but medications can be prescribed that help regulate these levels, which in turn helps regulate psychotic behaviors associated with bipolar disorder.

DT: *Well,* I think calling bipolar disorder a disease or illness can also imply that someone with the disorder is weak, vulnerable or inferior due to our society's associations with those words, "disease" and "illness." I am far from weak, vulnerable or inferior. I am bipolar, which is a mood disorder; is that so hard to say?

JP: No, but to be honest Derek I'm not really seeing how that reasoning is adding up to how bipolar disorder is *not* illness either. And there are a lot of people fighting out there that would disagree with you.

DT: This is how I fight the stigmas I feel in my life and is by no way the only way to fight and I understand that we all fight differently. Maybe in the future my opinion will change with more experiences, but I have yet to experience anything of the sort yet. I just don't feel like *I have* an illness.

KEY TERMS: JIMMY V, SOCIAL EXPERIMENT, 3. CRY, VIRGINITY
Submitted on 7/16/09
Green

Right now, my life is pretty hectic, so I was only able to catch around four or so hours of the Jimmy V charity event spread out on all of the ESPN networks yesterday. I was insanely jealous of the guy who had the winning bid for the ESPN College Football Game Day on Campus Experience. My reasons for this can be boiled down to two simplistic actions I would perform if I had won the bid:

1.)   When I got to deliver the mascot head to Corso on set, I would definitely throw the Heisman pose/hand into Desmond's (dick) face during the exchange.

2.)   When I got the chance to meet with the guys during the morning production meeting, I would persuade them that during the game picks segment, they must also pick their favorite sign in the crowd. I mean, it's only fair to recognize those people who worked so hard on cleverly insulting their opponent's city, school, family and girlfriends.

I was able to take something of value away from my vegetative state of watching radio on TV. This, of course, is the following quote from Jimmy V:

> To me, there are three things we all should do every day. We should do this every day of our lives. Number one is laugh. You should laugh every day. Number two is think. You should spend some time in thought. And number three is, you should have your emotions moved to tears, could be happiness or joy. But think about it. If you laugh, you think, and you cry, that's a full day. That's a heck of a day. You do that seven days a week, you're going to have something special.

After hearing this, I sat in contemplation for a while and reflected on what I thought was the meaning behind what Jimmy was trying to convey here. After this deliberation, I decided to try a social experiment on myself (it's not like I'm doing much else right now) and while I wasn't really all about trying this for an entire week, I figured one day of doing all three couldn't be too tough. After going through my day following Jimmy's words of wisdom, I figured I could determine if I had experienced something special (my mom always said I was special, kind of ironic, thinking about everything now) and write about it. So next, I pulled my best impersonation of Earl Hickey and started a list:

1. Laugh

2. Think

3. Cry.

Then after I spellchecked my list, I realized that I had already completed number 2 (remember "I sat in contemplation") so I crossed it off my list. ~~2. Think~~. Very nice.

My next to-do for the day was to either cry or laugh, two things I've perfected since my episode, so I thought this should be a piece of giant cookie. I should clarify: I'm not a huge fan of cake, so we always had giant chocolate chip cookies from the mall for my birthday growing up. AMC was running *History of the World: Part I* so I figured a laugh was pretty much guaranteed. While I did giggle slash cackle slash chuckle slash snicker, I didn't wholeheartedly laugh like I think Jimmy was referring to, so I couldn't cross that off my list.

At this point in the evening, I jumped into the shower, as I needed to start getting ready to venture down to the KY for some elegant riverfront dining (OK, it was Hooters, but they do have really good burgers, I'm told). During my shower routine, I enjoy listening to tunes, and one of the songs that randomly played was Ryan Adam's "Rescue Blues." For some reason, since my episode, that song messes with my emotions. ~~3. Cry~~. -

Well, it was nearing the end of the night and I hadn't yet laughed, so I was becoming a bit concerned. I sat down at J.B. Fins, totally disgusted with myself. I had been so close to completing my social experiment but was now convinced I'd fall short of my goal, and the culprit was laughter. The last time I checked, humor was in the title of this blog; pathetic.

Doesn't it seem like when you're lower than low, that's when everything starts to come together? At about that time in the night, on stage, Kevin Fox said these few words:

"So this song is about me in high school not being able to get laid. It's called 'Doesn't Do It.'"

I instantly started to crack up (it hit real close to home) and continued laughing through the entire song. ~~1. Laugh~~. Jimmy V was right. I really hadn't done anything throughout the day, but it was a full day.

SESSION

JP: God, I remember the first time I lost my virginity; it was by no means beautiful or in any way special.

DT: Please stop, I don't want to know any more about this because I'm pretty sure it will only make me feel even worse about my V-Card.

JP: Too bad, you get to vent all the time and now it's my turn. It was my freshman year in high school in my neighbor's shed, with a fellow band member who played the flute, named Helen. And let's just say polyester band uniforms back then were not the most breathable material, and things got really hot and really sticky really quickly.

DT: Yep, I was right; even though that's pretty gross, I'm still jealous. It's probably due to the fact that you lost your virginity to a girl well before me, and you don't *even like* girls.

KEY TERMS: MOPPING UP FOOLS, NKOTB, *THREE SHEETS*, BE MYSELF
Submitted on 7/21/09
Green

I'm not sure about other people, but there are essentially two times that I ever really get the desire to cut a rug, bring the funk, or otherwise showcase (or not) my skills of dance. The first of these two usually has slim to no consequences after said demonstration of dance moves, and that's when I'm totally alone. When I think I'm alone, I'm usually correct on that assumption, but there are two exceptions to the rule.

The first exception happened my freshman year in college, when I had just transferred from Marietta College up to Wittenberg for a multitude of reasons that really have no relevance to this story, so I'll tuck those away for a rainy day. I transferred mid-year and had only been at Witt for about a week and didn't know many people aside from a few in my classes. Like any other normal NKOTB, I wanted to make a good first impression whenever I could.

So I was on my way back down to Marietta the first weekend of the spring semester (my first at Witt) to grab some things I had left, when I came to the realization that I was alone in my Jeep (Jeep Wave) so I began bringing my funk via Nelly's "Luven

Me"; interesting song choice, I know. I was dominating that front seat with my moves for a good few minutes or so when I looked over at the car next to me at the stoplight--busted. Laughing hysterically at me was a very attractive girl from my psychology class. Awesome first impression.

During my entire day in the San Jose airport, awaiting my return flight back to the Emerald City, there were some interesting things going on in my head, and one of those things was a feeling of oneness or wholeness or some sort of connectivity with everything. To express this feeling, I was "lucky enough" to find an observation deck attached to the terminal outside the airport, where I could go to dance. Most people probably use it to watch the planes fly in or take smoke breaks, but where's the fun in that?

I spent a good hour or so (not too sure how long as the feeling of timelessness set in again) busting my moves on the top of that observation deck, pausing only for inbound and outbound planes. No one was around, so I felt totally comfortable with the display of random body convulsions known as my dance moves. I'm sure the video surveillance tape of me "dancing" on the observation deck is a cult classic at all of the San Jose airport's holiday parties.

The other times I feel like dancing are when I am *Three Sheets* (great show, BTW) to the wind. When I'm at the point in the night where I forget my name, chances are I'm on the dance floor mopping up fools, in a manner of speaking. Other than the few times when I almost got into fights (with groups of girls, big of me, I know) I cannot recall a night when I ended up in a dance-off; or a time when jamming out while cruising down the road wasn't fun. The only times I feel awkward or embarrassed are when I get caught: that exact moment when my comfort level drastically drops, due to my perception that someone else really cares about what I'm doing.

When I think about it later, I'm pretty sure they don't care. I know it shouldn't matter if I look like a fool to someone else, because why should I care? But I think that's just human. I care what my peers think because I'm part of them; it's a form of connection. Being part of this connection, I shouldn't worry about the people judging me from the wall or the ones laughing in the car next to me, but rather the ones challenging me to my next dance-off and dancing alongside me. I'm working on trying to be more like myself, and I think a part of that is not putting so much weight on what other people think of me. If I can do that, I might never stop dancing; another example of something that is good for me and even better for humanity.

SESSION

JP: I've worked in the past with some individuals who also have experienced timelessness in their mania, so this seems to be a fairly common symptom. Many of them seek answers in other places, such as spirituality. They read and relate to works by Dr. Stan Grof, Ken Wilber, R. D. Laing and C. G. Jung. Have you heard of these writers or any of their books?

DT: Yeah, I've read some Grof and Laing, but I found *The Science of Mind* by Ernest Holmes pretty interesting. It even inspired me to attend a spiritual service at my own free will.

JP: Did you only attend that one service?

DT: Yeah, well the service was on Sunday morning. That's right after Saturday night, man. I mean, who thought that was a good idea?

JP: Unpopular and boring people did . . . Well, if I wasn't going to hell, I surely am now.

DT: Ah, naw, you were definitely already going to hell.

KEY TERMS: "NORMAL," B-DAY GAME, WOODY HARRELSON, HER WILL
Submitted on 7/23/09
Green

As part of my recovery plan last year after my episode, I moved home to try to figure everything out. It was late summer, and my days consisted of getting up at the crack of ten or eleven in the morning; even then, it was a process to drag my butt out of bed. Then I took my six pills to become "normal" and sank into a TV-watching coma that lead to passing out on the couch for another hour or so. I'd get up and eat dinner, take another six pills to maintain my mood (drugged) and eventually pass out an hour or so later for the night. All in all, I was only getting around fifteen hours of sleep a day, the epitome of unproductivity. To try and counter this, I started working at my college job again, sealcoating blacktops; nothing too serious, but nonetheless a step. During lunches, we used to play the best game, and I'm bringing it to you now (thank me later): the Birthday Game.

Here's how it works. I'll go ahead and list a number of celebrities/famous peeps whose birthday is today, and you then try to guess their ages (*the answer key is at the bottom, but no cheating because you're only cheating yourself). Here we go:

1.) Nomar Garciaparra

2.) Monica Lewinsky

3.) Woody Harrelson

4.) Eriq La Salle

5.) Philip Seymour Hoffman

6.) Gary Payton

7.) Daniel Radcliffe

8.) Don Imus

9.) Slash

10.) My mom

Yes, today is the birthday of my mom, and this year I wanted to do something really cool and original for her. Over the past few months, my parental units have sort of caught up to the twenty-first century and begun using their phone for more than just talking--yes, texting. How freaked out are you when you get a text from your parents for the first time? I'm still recovering.

Since my mom has decided to take advantage of the multiple functions on her phone, I decided I was going to send her a birthday text. As I do with many of my friends, I texted the opening lyrics to 50 Cent's "In Da Club." She either didn't get the text or didn't know how to respond.

I was in quite a dilemma and had to act fast on my feet, so I booked it over to Target and started to frantically look over the b-day cards for that perfect one. You know, the one that someone else wrote but encompasses exactly what you were thinking, thereby allowing you to put as little thought as possible into that card; but I never found it.

Currently, my mom does not know I'm writing this blog, due to the fact I haven't told her. I'm not sure of the exact reason why I haven't, but I think I was trying to protect her in some weird way. I can't imagine what my family and friends are going through, trying to figure BMD out with me, but I think I have a little idea for my mom. We haven't been the most emotional family in the world. Three boys growing up together in the fields doesn't lead to sharing our feelings every night at dinner. That time was spent making fun of each other.

So when I got diagnosed with BMD, there was a learning curve for all of us. I would like to imagine that for Mom, it's kind of like a peewee football coach waking up one day to read in the paper that he's the new head football coach for the local professional football team. Sure, the coach knows football, but he's probably a little overwhelmed because his skills are not at the level that's needed to run a professional team; and for that matter, he didn't even apply for the job.

There's one thing I got from my mom that I know will get us through this just fine: her will. My mom is the strongest woman I know, and there's no way we all could handle this without her. I just wanted to say thanks for that, Mom, and don't worry about me. I'm going to be OK.

Happy Birthday.

(BTW, I did send my mom the link to this blog so she can read it now)

*1.) 36 (I'm still jealous of him for Mia Hamm)
2.) 36 (I'm still jealous of her for Bill Clinton)

3.) 48

4.) 47 (Just let your soooouuuuul glow, baby)

5.) 42

6.) 41 (The Glove; gotta be one of my Top 5 NBA nicknames ever)

7.) 20

8.) 69

9.) 44

10.) (Like there's any chance in hell I'm telling you that, I like my life and don't want it to end)

SESSION

DT: I hadn't read this one in a while. I like it a lot and forgot how many awesome celebs my mom shares her birthday with.

JP: Hello, Mom? It's John-Paul, sorry I haven't called in a while . . .

KEY TERMS: FORTUNE COOKIE, HILLBILLY ROAD TRIP, STALL GUY, ARCA

Submitted on 8/3/09

Green

I once read in a fortune cookie that in order to know where you are going, you must understand where you have been. Currently, in my day-to-day life, I'm in a transition period as I've decided to totally switch career paths and venture back to school. Having this opportunity to start over, I decided to take a mini vacation over the past week to try to reconnect with my past and hopefully pave the way for my future (don't get too impressed as I have yet to tell you what I actually did). I had a few options to choose from for my vacation destinations, including a trip down South to the beach and a venture out West to the mountains. While both of these destinations would have proved to be great getaways, I knew I needed to dig a little deeper into my past in order to get the results the cookie's fortune had revealed. A hillbilly road trip was my only true vacation destination.

As any experienced traveler knows, it is always a good idea to have at least one other person along with you on road trips; remember, safety in numbers. To begin my weeklong travels, I had one of my good friends, JD (BTW, I'm only using his initials to protect his identity because I never asked his consent to use his full name) accompany me to the first vacation destination, The Brickyard 400. Yes, that is a NASCAR race and yes, I know, it's a perfect way to start a hillbilly road trip.

Since I can remember, my family has been involved in racing in some form or another. Sponsorships, pit crews, dates, fans; you get the point. While a majority of these may have been in the ARCA series, I think the link to NASCAR is close enough. Our seats for the Brickyard were in the penthouse (not as glamorous as it sounds, turns out they're just on the top of the grandstands) going into turn one across from Johnson's pit. From our angle, we could see all of the front stretch, turn one, into turn two, and a short distance into the back stretch. I know I'm losing most of you, so I'll get to the point: our seats were amazing. Not because you could see so much of the track, but because the beer was only like ten steps to our left, and the bathroom was back and like five steps to our right, perfect. Because Cousin Carl (he's really not my cousin) was running in the middle to back of the pack most of the day, I needed to find a way to entertain myself. I found it in the bathroom.

There are a few behaviors that occur in a men's bathroom that I have always found unusual, odd, and flat out hilarious. One of these is when a grown-ass man uses the public urinal and pulls his pants all the way down to his ankles. Let me tell you, as the guy pissing right beside the grown-ass man, when he pulls this stunt, it brings about a feeling that is almost indescribable, but I'll try. For some reason, I start out feeling embarrassed for the bare-ass fellow and then confused, as I wonder how in the hell he never managed to notice the whole time he grew up that no one else pisses with their pants completely down. Then I feel uncomfortable for staring at this grown man's bare ass, all the while trying not to laugh at the whole situation.

Since shirts are optional at NASCAR races, I walked into the bathroom to see a fully naked grown-ass hillbilly standing at the urinal, pissing and smoking a Red. (That whole thing was pretty much a lie, but how amazing would that have been?)

The second behavior I simply call Stall Guy. This is when a guy waits in the bathroom line but refuses his turn and signals to us others to use the urinal (or three-man trough in Indy's Speedway case) so that he can wait for a more secure and comfortable stall. As I mentioned, Carl wasn't running real well, so I had some time to kill and decided to pull a stunt. I waited in line until it was my turn at the trough, and it just happened to be at full capacity with three men deep, so I knew my trap was set. The man at the far end finished up, and being next in line, I signaled to the man behind me to take the empty spot. He thought I was a Stall Guy; it's a known behavior in men's bathrooms. Next, the spot closest to the stalls opened, and the next guy behind me jumped in after observing my signaling with the previous man.

The 750 or so horsepower engines' noise bounces off the metal grandstands in the speedway, making it damn near impossible to talk during races, even in the bathroom. Everything had to be communicated through signals; of course, until I got to the trough. The middle spot opened, and I jumped right to it, started pissing and tried to start conversations with the two guys I signaled in before me on my left and right. You want to talk about uncomfortable situations: the looks on these hillbilly's faces as they realized the Stall Guy deliberately waited in line to get in the middle position between them in the trough, and then my trying to talk to them (or "hit on them" when they retell this story) was as great as a fully naked grown-ass hillbilly man standing at the urinal, pissing and smoking a Red. Maybe not, but close.

TBC . . .

SESSION

JP: Kick the tires and light the fires, boys!
DT: Are we flying jets or something, Maverick?
JP: Rubbin's racing!
DT: There you go, Cole Trickle.

KEY TERMS: SMOOTH CRIMINAL, LOST, PUSS, 2.6 PERCENT OF POPULATION
Submitted on 8/26/09
Green

I never thought these words would come out of my mouth, but I'm actually excited for school. Don't get me wrong; I used to get pumped to go to Miami View Elementary and check out who was in my class from the class assignments posted on the front doors at the end of summer, but that's a bit different. I've recently started classes here in The Nasty for my graduate degree, and for the first time in a while, I'm happy. Stubby and I headed out to lunch yesterday, and we were talking about how as long as you are doing something you enjoy, it doesn't seem like work.

I've talked about how bizarrely unpredictable this world is. One more piece of evidence: growing up in South Chuck, I never would have thought that I'd be able to live around the world and across the U.S. BMD has totally changed my life, sometimes for the bad, but mostly for the good. I've started over from scratch, and I've learned some valuable lessons and a lot about myself along the way. Today, I feel more like myself than I have in a long time. There's nothing fun about totally losing who you are.

Since my episode, I've looked at my journey back to myself as having some bumps in the road, and then at times being smoother than a criminal (my favorite MJ song; still a fan despite his legal issues, I think). There are too many things that I know I enjoy to list, but I can tell you of three that I absolutely do not like or have a desire to try: motorcycles (I'm a puss, I guess), shooting something dead (double puss), and going through depression again (just the word depression sounds awful).

Now, for the motorcycle and shooting something dead activities, I'll go ahead and group them together under P for puss, which allows me to write about them at the same time. My brother, stepdad, mom and aunts are motorcycle enthusiasts, so it should run in my blood, but it doesn't. I have never been on a motorcycle, and despite the attempts of the fam to have me take a ride on one (something weird about two guys on a bike that doesn't sit right with me, I'm not sure of the proper hand placement in this situation and not too thrilled to try and find out) I never will. I know that I have zero, nil, nix, nada, naught need to be on a bike (I bet you liked that alliteration).

Poncho would be the killing-things enthusiast in the family, or hunter if you want to be a dick about it. Don't get me wrong. I have no problems with hunters, other than the fact that hunting was an excused absence from school growing up; what a country! But it's another one of those experiences I could do without and feel I lived a pretty full life. I take Ron White's philosophy that if you have to get up early and it's cold, wet and dark, I don't want to do it. Despite my disdain for these recreational activities, I do understand the appeal to those who partake in them. This next one, I don't know anyone who likes it.

For the longest time, I looked at depression as someone being down on their luck and maybe needing to just look on the brighter side of life. I couldn't have been more off on that assumption (made an ass out of myself just like the old saying goes). Since I can remember, I've always been a pretty lighthearted fellow who never got down or felt anything but happy. Even in tough times, I'd try to look for the positive. TPO, Team Positively Optimistic member here. I don't know if it was my mind and body trying to put themselves back into balance after my episode or what, but I went through depression and it was the worst time of my life.

The feelings of worthlessness, of being pathetic, of hopelessness, and pure disgust at myself were almost more than I could handle. I may get a little annoyed with my mania from time to time, but I would take it over depression tenfold; I know I couldn't live with it. I've read that with BMD cases, a majority of females are on the depressed end of the spectrum, opposite of me, and my heart goes out to them. They are stronger than I could ever be.

I've learned from all of this that judgment, while it may be an implicit function of being human, is something I have to work on overcoming every day. It's beyond unfair to cast judgements about someone or something that I cannot, and more than likely am fortunate enough, not to have to experience (whether that be a single occurrence or a regularity in daily life). I would ride a motorcycle with three men at the same time while picking off squirrels with a .22 (or whatever the hell you shoot with a .22) before I'd make the choice to go through depression again.

SESSION

JP: Just for a little bit of clarification, I've put together some statistics about bipolar disorder that I'd like to share with you.

DT: Holy shit, you made a hand-out? Above and beyond, JP!

Bipolar Disorder Statistics

Who is Affected by Bipolar Disorder?

- Bipolar disorder affects approximately 5.7 million adult Americans or about 2.6 percent of the U.S. population age 18 and older every year. (National Institute of Mental Health)

- The median age of onset for bipolar disorder is twenty-five years (National Institute of Mental Health), although the illness can start in early childhood or as late as the forties and fifties.

- An equal number of men and women develop bipolar illness, and it is found in all ages, races, ethnic groups and social classes.

- More than two-thirds of people with bipolar disorder have at least one close relative with the illness or with unipolar major depression, indicating that the disease has a heritable component. (National Institute of Mental Health)

Women and Bipolar Disorder

- Although bipolar disorder is equally common in women and men, research indicates that approximately three times as many women as men experience rapid cycling. (*Journal of Clinical Psychiatry* 58, (1995): [Suppl. no. 15])

- Other research findings indicate that women with bipolar disorder may have more depressive episodes and more mixed episodes than do men with the illness. (*Journal of Clinical Psychiatry* 58, (1995): [Suppl. no. 15])

Economic Factors

- Bipolar disorder is the sixth leading cause of disability in the world. (World Health Organization)

Suicide and Bipolar Disorder

- Bipolar disorder results in 9.2 years reduction in expected life span, and as many as one in five patients with bipolar disorder complete suicide. (National Institute of Mental Health)

Children and Adolescents

- Bipolar disorder is more likely to affect the children of parents who have the disorder. When one parent has bipolar disorder, the risk to each child is 15 to 30 percent. When both parents have bipolar disorder, the risk increases to 50 to 75 percent. (National Institute of Mental Health)

- Bipolar disorder may be at least as common among youth as among adults. In a recent NIMH study, one percent of adolescents ages fourteen to eighteen were found to have met criteria for bipolar disorder or cyclothymia in their lifetime. (National Institute of Mental Health)

- Approximately 20 percent of adolescents with major depression develop bipolar disorder within five years of the onset of depression. (Birmaher, B., "Childhood and Adolescent Depression: A Review of the Past 10 Years, Part I," *Journal of the American Academy of Child and Adolescent Psychiatry*, 35, no. 11 [1996]: 1427-1439)

- Up to one-third of the 3.4 million children and adolescents with depression in the United States may actually be experiencing the early onset of bipolar disorder. (American Academy of Child and Adolescent Psychiatry, 1997)

- When manic, children and adolescents, in contrast to adults, are more likely to be irritable and prone to destructive outbursts than to be elated or euphoric. When depressed, there may be many physical complaints such as headaches, stomachaches or tiredness; poor performance in school, irritability, social isolation, and extreme sensitivity to rejection or failure. (National Institute of Mental Health)

Getting Treatment for Bipolar Disorder

- Success rates of 70 to 85 percent were once expected with lithium for the acute phase treatment of mania; however, lithium response rates of only 40 to 50 percent are now commonplace. (Surgeon General Report for Mental Health])

- Participation in a Depression and Bipolar Support Alliance (DBSA) patient-to-patient support group improved treatment compliance by almost 86 percent and reduced in-patient hospitalization. (DBSA, 1999)

- People with bipolar disorder face up to ten years of coping with symptoms before getting an accurate diagnosis, with only one in four receiving an accurate diagnosis in less than three years. (DBSA, 2000)

- A gender bias exists in the diagnosis of bipolar disorder: women are far more likely to be misdiagnosed with depression, and men are far more likely to be misdiagnosed with schizophrenia. (DBSA, 2000)

- Nearly nine out of ten people with bipolar disorder are satisfied with their current medication(s), although side effects remain a problem. (DBSA, 1999)

- People who report high levels of satisfaction with their treatment and treatment provider have a much more positive outlook about their illness and their ability to cope with it. (DBSA, 1999)

JP: I'd like to thank the Depression and Bipolar Support Alliance website at http://www.dbsalliance.org for this information.

DT: Many thanks for that acknowledgement, JP. I really don't wanna get sued for copyright infringement. I mean, I know the slander and defamation of character suits are on the way, so I'd like to limit my legal issues as much as possible.

KEY TERMS: *HIGHLIGHTS*, EMPTINESS, PRIVACY, THE CIVIL WAR
Submitted on 9/8/09
Green

I think you can make a pretty accurate judgment on what kind of experience you are in for from the selection of reading material in a waiting room. As much as I hated going to the dentist growing up, having those *Highlights* magazines there to entertain me during the minutes leading up to the oral misery made the trip seem not so bad. While awaiting my turn in the barbershop chair, I can always count on getting caught up on my sports with *SI*, *ESPN the Magazine* and other sports-themed mags (and the occasionally skimming-through of *Glamour* is purely accidental, mind you).

While working in my sales job in The Nasty, I would from time to time be on appointments in which I was forced to wait until my contact was available to meet. During those times, I could be found browsing through periodicals about hunting, cars, the Civil War, politics, and television. Each of these themes would mentally prepare me, good or bad, for the encounter I was about to undertake. I'm not sure whether this quirk of mine is shared by others, but I somehow tried to envision the person and experience I was about to undergo based upon that material sitting out in the waiting room.

Imagine my complete dumbfoundedness (yeah, obviously not a word since I get that red squiggly line under it after I type it, but I'm keeping in all the same) when I walked into the Mental Health and Psychiatry Department of THE Ohio State University Harding Hospital and found but one magazine in the waiting room. It was so awful, I can't even remember what genre I would try to categorize it under. This wasn't a good start for me.

At this point in my life, I had made the trek back from the mountains to settle into the familiar flat farming fields of central Ohio; I was home. While I really didn't know if I wanted or thought I needed to see a psychiatrist or psychologist, I felt so lost and confused with this whole thing that I agreed to go, partly to entertain my parents' wishes, partly to look for answers, and partly because I felt it was the responsible thing to do. Granted,

I did not have the best experience with my medical care in Denver. But that was probably due to the fact that at the time, I could not come to terms with the BMD diagnosis and therefore felt that I was not different and did not need any help--strike one. However, after hearing that my mom had gotten me into THE Ohio State University Harding Hospital, even though I had no referral and the wait list was about six months, I figured it was a good thing. She has a gift for persuasion; some would use other terms to describe it, but it's definitely a gift.

Sitting in the waiting room with nothing to read and no idea of what my doc looked like, I kept pulling the fake stand-up move whenever someone would walk by and make eye contact with me. Finally, a shorter man with glasses and a beard walked into the room and beckoned me to follow. I figured I had nothing to lose, so I followed.

We entered his office, and I asked if he was doc so-and-so (that wasn't really his name, but I'm a man of ethics and decided to respect his privacy) and he replied yes. He explained to me that he didn't use names in the waiting room for confidentiality reasons. I didn't get it. I was in the mental health hospital at THE Ohio State University. It's safe to say the majority of people around me had a good idea of why I was there, but que-evs, it was a nice gesture nonetheless.

He opened the conversation by asking me to tell him what happened and who I was in a nutshell (that's ad lib, he really didn't say nutshell). I was a little set back because I wasn't sure how to answer. For some reason, I felt embarrassed and uncomfortable in this procedural-like interview process. It felt almost as if the doc had a standard set of questions to ask with no real interest in the answers, only that there was an answer so that he could make his way to the next question. I started out by telling him my name, where I was from, where I went to school, what I had been doing with my life, and recalling as many details from my episode as I could. It did get easier to talk to the doc as the conversation continued, but I never felt comfortable with it.

I felt ashamed of myself for what had happened, and nothing about being in that office made me feel any differently. That was probably my fault. Just as I had no expectations from the lack of reading material in the waiting room, the feelings of no expectation were the same in the office: there wasn't any chemistry between us. While these feelings of emptiness were out of my control, I could have handled the situation better.

I ended up heading back a few times to Harding Hospital, but then I took a job in The Nasty and stopped my meetings with the doc. I wouldn't all together change anything in my life, but at times I do wish I had done a few things differently. If I could do over that initial meeting, I would walk in with my head high, chest out, and a smile on my face and started out by saying:

"My name is Derek Thompson. I was raised in South Charleston, Ohio and was recently diagnosed with bipolar disorder type I; which is considered a mental illness by some, but I wouldn't have it any other way. This is my story . . ."

SESSION

JP: Getting treatment for bipolar disorder is not a one-time effort. Bipolar disorder is a chronic illness, meaning that people with the disorder need to take medication and visit with their doctors routinely for their entire lives. Here are some questions that may help you decide on the right doctor or other health care professional for you:

- Do you feel comfortable when you are with this person?

- Do you respect this person's knowledge?

- Do you trust this person's judgment?

- Do you believe this person will do his or her best to help you get well?

- Does this person seem to listen to your concerns?

- Does this person try to answer your questions in a way you understand?

- Is the office staff helpful when you make an appointment, ask a question, or need to contact your health care professional?

Finding a health care professional you trust, and who makes you feel comfortable, may make following your treatment plan easier.

DT: Damn, that's good advice, JP. Where were you two years ago when I needed that?

JP: Oh, I see how you are; only interested in my past when it could have benefited you.

DT: Derr.

KEY TERMS: TIME TRAVEL, NEGLIGENT, "IF," SOLDIER FOR THE LIGHT
Submitted on 9/15/09
Green

Seeing how the NFL kicked off its season last week, I feel I have an obligation to cover some aspect of the opening weekend. I think they would revoke my Man Card if I didn't. Seeing how I'm not one to sit and analyze the games, I've decided to give you a couple of points to ponder from my NFL opening week observations.

Numero uno is that I am no longer on speaking terms with the city of Denver. This is a bit sad to admit, as I always felt like our relationship would somehow rebound after the episode, but it is evident Denver wants nothing to do with me. I knew we were in trouble after I found the city to be negligent (can you tell I'm taking a law class in grad school or what?) after my episode, but I retained hope that someday we could make up and be happy again. While I was open to trying this, Denver obviously had different intentions, as evidenced when the Broncos ripped my heart out and wiped their butts with it in the play I'm simply calling "The Tip" (I refuse to go into more detail because it hurts too much).

Next, I've always thought it would be hilarious and downright fun to have a little person (I'm pretty sure that is PC but if not, to the five people who read this blog, I'm sorry if I offended you) dress up in the same outfit that I was wearing and follow me around for a day. I wouldn't acknowledge the creepiness involved or that they were even there, despite the fact I would have them mimic my every move. However, it was pointed out to me that I would simply be ripping off the intellectual property (another law term; on fire) of Mike Myers, and I don't want to get on the bad side of any Canadian (I like our Northern neighbors) so I dropped the idea.

So, inspired by the NFL kickoff week, I've decided that I would want to hire one of the "professional" water boys of the NFL to follow me around for a day. I'd have them dress up in green and black, wear .e4 gear along with my logo (that's the thing to the right on the blog, we'll get to that one day as well, once again please try to control your excitement). Every so often, when I'm thirsty, I'd blow a whistle and stop the clock for a timeout and have them run over and squirt water into my mouth while they covered my chin with a towel. A little weird, but so refreshing.

OK, now that I feel I've done my due diligence as a man to comment on football this past weekend, I'll go ahead and talk a little bit about what brought me to those observations. My stepdad made his way down to The Nasty this weekend as we had plans to attend a fly fishing school on Saturday and the Bengals game on Sunday; all in all a nice weekend, despite the misery associated with being an Ohio football fan. I've also since decided that I'm jumping on the UC Bearcats bandwagon because I figure if all the Ohio Steelers fans can be fair weather fans, why can't I?

To start out the weekend, on Friday night we decided to try a local Brazilian steakhouse downtown, and it was the bomb diggity (that means good). During the endless plates of meat, we got to talking and stumbled upon the topic of what I think would have happened if I never moved to Denver and stayed in the ATL. I had never given much thought to the idea because I felt that what happened was destined to happen, no matter where I was. I've become a firm (ha-ha, I said firm, shouts out to my Southern sis) believer that everything works out like it's supposed to. And even if something strange, unpredictable, terrible or horrific happens to you (say you believe you're a soldier for the light, fighting against the darkness of evil to protect a sacred blood line, or something to that effect) it's what you do afterwards that defines you as a person.

We continued our discussion, dissecting the "if" scenarios of staying in the ATL. "If you were in the ATL, do you think it would have happened?" "If you were in the ATL, do you think the episode would have been as severe?" "If you were in the ATL, do you think the episode would have lasted as long?" "If you were in the ATL, would you have worn long hair that was combed to the side, boat shoes, short khaki shorts, and sunglasses with Croakies?" (OK, that didn't really come up in conversation, but I had to take a little jab at the Southern boys, still got nothing but love for ya, though.) After some serious thought, I still don't know the answers to those "if" questions, but I do know one thing that resounds in me. When I focus too much on the "ifs" in the world, I am missing out on so much more, because they actually are just part of my life.

SESSION

DT: I never understood Croakies in Atlanta. What, are your shades going to fly off your face so fast that you lose them as you walk down Peachtree Street/Battle/Road/whatever?

JP: I think it's probably more of a style or trend than anything else.

DT: Oh, my blunder.

KEY TERMS: HOKEY POKEY, BUMPER STICKERS, SELF-IMAGE, THE MASS
Submitted on 10/14/09
Green

Fat Chicks Rule

This was the bumper sticker that I was staring at as I made my way into town on Friday. Some people absolutely love these cleverly revealing stickers attached to vehicles, while others despise them. I am completely fascinated by them, although I have only had one in my life, and it was of a soccer ball, in high school (grass fairy). The soccer ball wasn't much of a statement and really didn't bother anyone, aside from the guys still questioning their sexuality and expressing their frustration by calling me gay for playing soccer (you know you are) so I was OK with it. Some people find bumper stickers tacky, cheap, obnoxious, and downright pathetic. But let me tell you why they fascinate me. I'll begin with a list of some of my faves:

- Gas, Ass or Grass. Nobody Rides for Free

- Dip Me in Beer and Throw Me to the Drunk Chicks

- I Support the Right to Arm Bears

- Nice Truck. Sorry About Your Penis

- --Caution--I Brake For Hookers

These have no real message to put out there, but I heart them. My reasoning behind this is that while the people sporting these stickers aren't trying to change the world, they are at least living in their own. These aren't words of wisdom or the key to life (well, maybe the sticker that reads, "What if the Hokey Pokey Really IS What it's All About?" has some insight) but they make me laugh and make my day a little better.

Prior to my episode, I think I was living my life for some of the wrong reasons. I strove to be good in high school because that's what I was supposed to do in order to go to college. In college, I tried to be the guy everyone liked, and I never wanted to step on anyone's toes. I got a job out of school with a big corporation and lived the mundane office life for a few years because that's what I was supposed to do. I never took a side or position on anything of importance because I didn't want to separate myself from the majority. I didn't have a bumper sticker because it wasn't what "respectable" people did.

It seemed like I was living my life for everyone else and not for myself most of the time. Despite the abundance of "No Fear" bumper stickers, I feared being different from my peers, being an individual. I cared so much about what other people thought that I'm not sure I knew exactly who I was. I can recall in college my girlfriend asking me who I was; a few cocktails deep, but a fair question nonetheless. I was absolutely crushed to think that my girlfriend lacked confidence in me, doubted me, and did not know me. I became defensive and felt betrayed by her (all the best to ya though, Jill [Radio Edit], and you were in my dream last night; weird). She was right. I didn't know who I was at that time. It only took a psychotic episode for me to figure that out, no big deal.

I've since tried to live my life the way I feel I should. I no longer fear not being accepted or liked or understood. Sure, I'm scared from time to time about BMD and what might happen because of it, but I'm not going to let it dictate my life and prevent me from being myself. In fact, it has allowed me to step out and find who I am. I no longer care nearly as much as I used to if someone doesn't like me or if they disagree with me; I enjoy it. I couldn't imagine a world where everyone liked each other because then we'd all be the same, and what's fun about that? In that crazy world, there'd only be one bumper sticker, and it would probably say something lame like, "Have a nice day." I'd rather know the opinion of the obese, drunk, crazy, obnoxious, prideful, straight, individualistic, liberal, atheist, spiritual, conservative, alternative life-styled, bastards and bitches of the world. It's just a lot more fun.

SESSION

JP: I think you hit on a subject here that many of us, both bipolar and not, can relate to. The struggle for self-confidence, self-esteem and self-image can torment many of us. A few tips to build upon could be: look towards a model to learn from; act like you are self-confident and you will be self-confident; always smile and stand up straight; and work on your relaxation skills. Have you had success with any of these in the past, Derek?

DT: Yeah, except my relaxation skills were to act like a confident prick while smiling to try and sleep with my model I was learning from.

JP: Don't forget to stand up straight afterwards, dick.

KEY TERMS: UNDERDOG, MANIA, BUNGLES, DEFENSE MECHANISM
Submitted on 3/22/10
Green

Professor X, this is nothing you asked for but everything you need (I promise this will eventually make sense).

"Welcome to AT&T's 'At The Half,' where you have just been watching the number one seeded Mania vs. the Cinderella story of number twelve seeded d01roK. I'm Greg Gumbel, and as always, seated beside me is the point guard of our team, Greg Anthony, and shut down man Seth Davis. Guys, we all went into this matchup expecting top-seeded Mania to run away with this game, but d01roK from rural Ohio refuses to go away. What have been the keys in this game thus far?"

"Well, Greg I've always said be wary of the underdog because they have nothing to lose and everything to gain. Right now, d01roK is playing with just that mentality. I can recall playing in games where we weren't the favorite, and there was always just a bit of a chip on your shoulder from this that can elevate your game. d01roK has found something inside himself that he's using to overcome the intensity and relentless pursuit of Mania. I'm not sure if he can hold onto it for the duration, but I think we're in for one heck of a show."

"Yeah, Greg is right on that, but I just feel the overwhelming talent that Mania has on its side, coupled with the experience of being around since the dawn of time, will play a factor in the second half. Don't get me wrong, it's great to see a Cinderella story like d01roK come out of nowhere to challenge a favorite, but I'm not sure he can hold on when the hallucinations and delusions come into play. That's been the forte of Mania, to wait till the second half and then really pour on the nasty."

"Well, one way or the other, we'll have a clearer picture of the outcome right after a word from our sponsors, and then we'll send you out to your game for the conclusion. Thanks for watching AT&T 'At The Half,' and enjoy the rest of the game."

This has become my defense mechanism of late to help cope with my mania. I have always rooted for the underdog since I can remember (please be aware, my fanhood really doesn't kick in until roughly the early '90s, so I've only known my favorite team as the Bungles). I'm not entirely quite sure why, but I've always related to them no matter the occasion. It could be that since I was five, I've participated in the only thing more foreign to country folk than public transportation--soccer--or that I always saw myself as a five-one, 100-pound immature freshmen throughout high school (not really the ladies' man) or that I felt like I never belonged to the Carhartt crew growing up (Adidas and Umbros here). Whatever the reason is, I'm starting to realize I'm glad it's there.

To me, a real underdog is a person or team that is fighting against the odds but refuses to acknowledge this. A real underdog doesn't fight for their life-- they fight because that's all they know how to do. A real underdog doesn't care about the spread, or fear their opponent, or listen to the experts but rather lives for the opportunity to prove themselves. A real underdog will be knocked down, beat up, kicked out, and stomped in time after time and still gets up and asks for more. This is because a real underdog isn't an underdog at all. They are exactly what they want to be.

My mania has left me beaten, alone, and crying on my bathroom floor, but I've gotten up. I know I'll be brought back down again, and it could be today or it could be in a few years. But I know one thing for sure: I'll never stop getting back up. My professor in my PR class (Professor X) asked us to write a blog about sports. She asked that we include hyperlinks and tags to ensure that our message is heard as much as possible. She wanted to see our voice come out in our writing and to make a footprint for ourselves through technological gadgets and online tricks. The problem is, I don't do this for the world to hear my message. I do this for me. So while I didn't give you exactly what you wanted, Professor X, I did give you what you needed: my voice. I am an underdog.

SESSION

JP: So how exactly does the mania leave you beaten, alone, and crying on your bathroom floor? Is it physically bringing you down to your knees with pain, or is this more of an emotional state of mind that drives you down from the mania?

DT: It's mainly an emotional thing with my mania. It will grab me and not let go. I'll dwell on how much I've lost in the fight, and the mania seems to thrive on this. I'm usually able to pull myself out of it after a few minutes, and since I've been taking lithium regularly, it hasn't been as bad.

JP: Oh, so staying on your medicine does seem to help. I guess we professionals *do* know what we're talking about.

DT: Easy with the liberal use of the term "we" in regard to medical professionals there, JP. I'm pretty sure you got your degree online.

JP: I know you're lashing out at your past failed healthcare relationships and not me, so I'm going to ignore that last comment, but I want you to know it did hurt a little bit.

KEY TERMS: ARCHNEMESIS, JAY CUTLER, WHO I AM, GUERILLA WARFARE
Submitted on 4/6/10
Green

Name: Jay Cutler
Position: QB
Number: 6
College: Vanderbilt University
Birthdate: 04/29/1983
Height/Weight: 6-3/233
Hobbies: Being My Archnemesis
Team: Chicago Bears

Throughout my life, there have been a number of guys along the way who inevitably became my archnemesis. I know that there will be arguments and grumblings that you can only have one archnemesis and that's it (mainly Star Wars and comic book nerds probably, low blow, I know). My dad never sat me down and had the archnemesis talk with me, so I had multiple archnemeses growing up. For instance, in my redshirt year of kindergarten, my address was my archnemesis, followed by my neighbor's black Star Wars Big Wheel and the McDonald's Big Mac Song records. Eventually, these evolved into actual guys in the third grade or so (you know who you are). Each of these archnemeses always seemed to fade into the background as the new one emerged. That is, until I received my internship in Chicago.

Jay Cutler has reappeared in my life after the time we spent together in Denver, and I'm not too pleased about it. Our first run-in was in the mountains, and the battle was as rugged as the Rockies. It was the summer of 2007, and I had been romantically involved with a girl who brought a little bit of home to Denver. She was a country girl who raced dirt bikes (BTW, they ride bikes, not drive them, I always screwed that up). We were out, basically owning the dance floor (I was the best dancer in the club Murph; just saying) when Jay walked in and proceeded to post up at the bar, and I knew it was on.

Jay attempted the guerrilla warfare tactic common among inferior challengers. His first strategy was to pretend that he didn't even know I existed; clever. Next, he attempted to court one of my good friends right underneath my nose; the audacity. Finally, he tried to pick up the girl (tiny ballerina now) I was dating while I sat home and watched the Reds. And this was in just one off-season when we both shared the same city, before my episode shipped me home.

I hadn't thought about having any archnemesis since my diagnosis because I felt like BMD was now the only enemy in my life. But I think that's a bad way to approach it. BMD is a part of me, and the good and the bad of it are who I am. I can't have myself as an archnemesis; I'd always win, and that's no fun. It looks like Jay will just have to do. I'm moving to Chicago, and the off-season is alive and humming in the NFL. I wonder what Jay has up his sleeves this time, because I heard he had a single sister.

SESSION

JP: I think your taking ownership of bipolar disorder and accepting it as part of you is a great step, and one that many people struggle with.

DT: It's definitely a difficult step to take, almost as tough as watching Jay Cutler score with Kristin Cavallari. Just when I thought my archnemesis couldn't be any more deviant, he steals away one of my TV Top Five--

JP: You didn't hear? They called off the wedding.

DT: Really . . . very, very interesting . . .

JP: I've seen that look before. Please try to limit your creepiness towards this poor girl. Oh no wait, wait just one second here. I'm double checking online and I think they just got back together . . . and now off again . . . and now back. . .

KEY TERMS: ABILIFY, NORMALCY, ALCOHOL PROHIBITION, LITHIUM
Submitted on 10/22/10
Green

Last week, a woman said to me those three little words that all single men fear:

"You're cut off."

Yes, my new doc has cut me off from the one thing I thought might provide some sort of normalcy in my life: alcohol. This wasn't due to my usage (I was pretty good at drinking it) but the fact that there have been instances of instant death when combining too much alcohol with lithium--could've known *that* eight months ago. Of course, when I asked how and why, I received the standard BMD medical response:

"We don't know."

And before anyone has to ask, I'm man enough to admit it: yes, I cried when they took it away (sucker punched my ass). I wasn't upset that I had to quit drinking--well, not cold turkey, but stick to a two-drink maximum--but that once again, something was being taken from me, and no one could tell me exactly why. I felt I had already given up so much in my life, and drinking was the last thing that was familiar to me. I liked being able to have some drinks with my friends and feel close to my old self.

Once I got that out, I felt better and made the wise decision to stop drinking and stay on my lithium (I like breathing a little more than drinking; just a little). I could have explored other medicines that would allow me to drink, but lithium seems to be working right now, and I'm not a big fan of fixing something that's not broke (hell, I can't fix something that *is* broke). Adding a new "medicine" to my system is an experience I'd like to limit as much as possible. The next time you see a commercial for the "medicine" Abilify, pay attention to the possible side effects. I was fortunate enough to have a majority of them. The involuntary spasms were wicked as hell.

After three years of what seemed like continuous failure, I feel things are starting to turn a bit. I've finally got insurance (I'm killing their bottom line but they have to play nice). My lithium levels are normal. I like my new doc and counselor (kind of a shocker) and my new job. My place is coming together, and I'll have a new vehicle very soon; the Toyota's 238K probably isn't reliable enough for a traveling sales job. If I have to trade some hangovers for all of that, that's fine by me.

On a lighter note, I used to pride myself on having clever or witty remarks about my Facebook page, purely for my own entertainment. When I moved out to the country, I didn't have Internet service for the first month or so. This didn't allow me to keep up with updates on my page, so in honor of the alcohol prohibition put on my life, I dedicated my page to the only girl I can still outdrink: Fisher.

This snake from the plains (a select few will get that) used to constantly barrage me in college with the challenge that every guy rolls his eyes at when he hears it coming from a girl:

"I can outdrink you!"

Of course I told her *she* drinks like a girl and accepted the challenge, and it was a close contest, I must admit. Up until the early point in the night when I was informed that she was under the ping pong table . . . she drinks like a girl, and so do I now.

SESSION

JP: I think it's a good idea to share some symptoms of lithium toxicity with the alcohol discussion going on here. The likelihood of toxicity increases with higher serum lithium levels. Serum lithium levels greater than 1.5 mEq/mL carry a greater risk than lower levels. However, patients sensitive to lithium may exhibit toxic signs at serum levels below 1.5 mEq/mL.

Diarrhea, vomiting, drowsiness, muscular weakness and lack of coordination may be early signs of lithium toxicity, and can occur at lithium levels below 2.0 mEq/mL. At higher levels, giddiness, ataxia, blurred vision, tinnitus and a large output of dilute urine may be seen. Serum lithium levels above 3.0 mEq/mL may produce a complex clinical picture involving multiple organs and organ systems.

Fine hand tremor, polyuria and mild thirst may occur during initial lithium therapy for the acute manic phase, and may persist throughout treatment. Transient mild nausea and general discomfort may also appear during the first few days of lithium administration. By the way, how's the no-drinking going? I was just wondering with all this lithium toxicity talk going on, ya know?

DT: I'm still here, so I'd say pretty good.

JP: That doesn't really answer my question, now, does it?

DT: Well, you definitely plagiarized your little speech there so let's just drop it.

JP: Fair enough.

KEY TERMS: WIMP, EUCHRE, SON-OF-A-BITCH, CHEATER
Submitted on 10/29/10
Green

I can count the number of times I've been in a fight on Stubby's left hand: 0. That's not to say I haven't had my run-ins, tiffs, quarrels, disagreements, confrontations, arguments or push-offs, but that's about where it ends. I suppose I've always figured that I would lose any fight I was in, so why even mess with the whole defeat aspect and avoid the fight altogether? Some say I'm a lover, not a fighter, or they call me a wimp. Maybe it was the scrawny build I had most of my life, maybe it was my fear of failure, maybe it was that I was faster than everyone else, or maybe I wasn't supposed to fight until now.

I'm really looking forward to the holidays that are coming up because I feel like I missed them last year, being manic and all for X-Mas and New Year's and building my way there at Thanksgiving. Growing up, my favorite part of the holidays wasn't the food, the live Nativity Scene reenactment, the gifts, the family stories; nope, none of that traditional stuff. I loved Euchre. My Southern friends, you'll have to Google that game and will probably hate on it (just like you hate on everything Yank, no worries, we do the same to the South anyway). Everyone else, you know what I'm talking about.

Nothing caps off the family get-together quite like being in the barn and milking those udders in front of your uncles. I have determined that there are two ways one can play Euchre, each effective in its own right. The first is the traditional honest, rule-fearing way that the majority of the world plays, and then there's the table talk, reneging, questionable method. I liked to play the latter; it's just a little more fun. Be easy on me, it's not totally my fault. It runs in the family. Right, Aunt Nene?

There have been some consequences for my cheating, and I'd like to share one of those times with everyone. The year was somewhere around the late nineties, and I was early into my hoop-earrings phase of my life. It was the Thompson Family Christmas (with live reenactment of the Nativity Scene, dibs on Joseph) and the games of Euchre were starting to heat up. Being the two oldest, Cuzin Jen and I of course teamed up (she's just an innocent bystander for the record) and were locked up against Aunt Nancy and her insignificant teammate for the point of this story. The game was close, and we squeaked out a couple point victory on a hand that I cheated with. Aunt Nancy was confused about how and why she lost the final hand, so I remarked with a smirk:

"Well, I've been reneging the whole time."

Aunt Nancy got fired up and lectured me before she stormed out of the room. She still refuses to play Euchre with me to this day.

It's crazy to think about sometimes, that I'm going to spend the rest of my life fighting something that is stronger, bigger, smarter, more experienced, craftier, and overall just a son-of-a-bitch that fights any way but fair. It makes me laugh to think that I avoided fights my entire life, and now I have to confront an opponent that is simply better than me for the rest of my life. It's probably a good thing I like to cheat.

SESSION

JP: You cheating S-O-B, you're the reason I got so hammered last weekend in those drinking games, aren't you?

DT: Hahahahahahahahahahaha, oh hahaha! Whew, no, I would never do that to you, JP.

KEY TERMS: LIBIDO, I <3 VAGINA, ACCEPTING, THANKSGIVING HUNT
Submitted on 11/24/10
Green

I am so thankful to have my libido back!

OK, now that we got that out of the way, in honor of Thanksgiving, let's get down to what's really important. I will soon be on my way down to Charlotte for Cuzin Jen's wedding, and I couldn't be more excited for those Southern belles, making a country boy from Ohio get down on his knees and beg for more. In honor of hunting season as well, and to celebrate my sex drive's return (so weird, I know) I'm going on a little hunt this weekend, and accompanying me on this epic adventure will be my wingman, brother, and all-around good guy, Poncho.

I spent eighteen months in Atlanta posing as an apprentice/account executive at AT&Tizzle to learn the culture and ways of the Southern belle. These women are so different from anything I've encountered in my life. They're nice and sweet more than once every three Saturdays, which means it'll take dedication, passion, balance and awareness (.e4 reference) to attract one of these beauties. We'll have our work cut out for us.

In preparation for the hunt, I spent last Friday out in The Nasty drinking a few (I'll explain the end to my own personal alcohol prohibition later, but it's basically just another trust issue with my docs) and casually watching my friends pull some random intoxicated girl into their car and speed away (don't worry, we found them at the next bar). As I mentioned, my libido has recently resurfaced, which is great for me and unfortunate for the single women within a sixty-mile radius of Grape Grove (BTW, I did think to try the singles night at the Grape Grove Church of Christ, not really the demographics I was looking for). For some unknown and unfair reason, whenever I'm manic or depressed or recovering from one of the two, I lose my sex drive. I'm still a man and do seize the moment if it arises, but my heart isn't really into it, which probably drops me from about a five to a three. This equates to about a few months in the past three years that my libido was alive and kicking.

I'm back in the game and have the bruises on my chest and nips from the "kidnap" victim mentioned earlier to prove it; she was such a giver. Now, I know the belles will not fall for anything close to that effort. I once had to spend seven months ignoring one just to get her to notice me; it was well worth it, though. I mean, this girl did have a sexy accent, and if she was from up here I would have had to fight off a dozen "bros" in bandannas with I <3 vagina t-shirts every time we went out. Yeah, she was smokin' hot. I used to have some "revealing" pictures to show said hotness, but I deleted them when I was manic; I know I hate myself, too.

Poncho's uncanny whimsical pickup lines and my keen knowledge of the Southern belle should provide us with an eventful trip down South. I'll be sure to let you all know how things turn out, but I have a real good feeling about this. I haven't felt this good in a while, almost like I'm finally accepting what I am supposed to be with this BMD, and I'm really glad it included my libido. I'm just hoping that if I am successful on my Thanksgiving hunt, the belle wants to keep the lights off; I don't know how I'd explain the bruises.

Happy Thanksgiving!

SESSION

DT: I got you a late birthday present, JP, here you go. Hope you like it.

JP: Thank you! Let's see, it's a . . . really? An I <3 Penis t-shirt, you *really* shouldn't have.

DT: Try it on, try it on . . .

KEY TERMS: PINEHURST, COSI, DUCKS, MOUNT VESUVIUS
Submitted on 12/3/10
Green

My Thanksgiving hunt was about as successful as my golfing: through twelve holes at Pinehurst, I lost ten balls, hit a barn, sent an old man with a bad hip running, and I mean *drilled* a house. The hunt was so unsuccessful that I even upset a follower of .e4; down to sixteen from seventeen. I must really be on my game.

Seeing how my game makes me laugh, I'm going to continue to share it with my now sixteen followers. As I previously mentioned, I decided to give the online dating scene a try. I figure I buy sneakers online for double the monthly price of the sites, so this is one hell of a deal. I'm beginning to realize I'm as bad at dating as I am at golf.

Maybe it's my approach, but I find it humorous to reveal my stats. Ten emails sent; zero replies. Zero emails received; one wink, but I think it was accidental. I managed to run off a girl whose number I received two years ago. No idea how I managed that one, considering I asked her out to COSI; yeah I know, great date idea. I was even blown off by a friend of a friend to whom I merely said hello and good luck (I'm totally stumped on that one). You can imagine how I'm beginning to doubt myself a little, which is highly unusual for me. Some say I have an air of confidence. Others simply call me a dick.

Because of this lack of success, I decided to really focus when I was going through the picture menu on Match.com (eat your heart out, Shoney's). I am looking for a tall blonde (shocker, I know, sis) who has a sense of humor ranked high because damn it, I'm funny. I thought I had found her: tall, blonde, into sports, ranks laughter extremely high and is studying child psychology. The last item was perfect because I act like a kid from time to time and I'm bipolar; we'd have tons to talk about. Once again, failure on my end, but it was funny, at least to me.

Here's how it went down:

Email 1

To: (Radio Edit)

Subject: Yeah, I'm emailing on Thanksgiving . . .

Body: Big whoop, wanna fight about it? I can't imagine how much shit you must catch on here for your screen name so big ups for staying true to that whore of a city up North (ha-ha I kid I kid).

Response: Nothing. She's a Michigan fan; I know, I know.

Email 2

To: (Radio Edit)

Subject: Stop me if you've heard this one before . . .

Body: We're on our way home from our first date (it went well) when we get into a horrific car accident. My brother (yeah, in order for the joke to work there needs to be three people, he likes you, though) and I are killed and are awaiting our entry into heaven. At the gate, St. Peter gives us the rundown of how things operate there in paradise. He points out the hot spots and warns us to steer clear of the ducks. See, those ducks are God's prized possessions and he would be enraged if anything happened to them. Well, I step up and decide that I'm going to just walk real cautiously and slowly, paying attention to every step in order to not harm the ducks. Wouldn't you know it, after three steps I step right on a duck, killing it and sealing my fate. St. Peter walks up and says, "You know, you're going to have to be punished for this," so I get handcuffed to the ugliest girl in heaven for all eternity (tough break). My brother steps up and just takes off in a dead sprint, balls to the wall running, and tramples a duck, killing it. St. Peter comes over, and since I already have the ugliest girl in heaven on my arm, the second ugliest is handcuffed to him for eternity. A few months pass by and my brother and I (with our hideous cuff mates) are walking around heaven when we catch a glimpse of you across the way. You're handcuffed to the Brad Pitt of angels in heaven, so we run over and ask:

"What happened? How in the hell are you handcuffed to that!?"

The Brad Pitt angel replies:

"I don't know, I just stepped on a damn duck."

Ha-ha-ha, anything? Anything? That's like from middle school humor, you gotta love that . . .

Response: Nothing.

Email 3

  To: (Radio Edit)

  Subject: My last try, I promise . . .

  Body: So obviously you're not into tall, dark, handsome and funny guys, so how about the adventurous type? Did I ever tell you the story about when I was rappelling down Mount Vesuvius when suddenly I slip, and I start to fall? Just falling, ahh ahh, I'll never forget the terror. When suddenly I realize: "Holy shit, Derek, haven't you been smoking peyote for six straight days, and couldn't some of this maybe be in your head?"

  "And?" you ask.

  And it was. I was totally fine. I've never even been to Mount Vesuvius.

  I'm Derek, and your name is?

  Response: Nothing (ha-ha).

Email 4 (Sent right after this entry)

  To: (Radio Edit)

  Subject: So I lied . . .

  Body: www.e4-d01rok.blogspot.com

  Response: TBC???

SESSION

JP: So, did you ever hear from her?

DT: Hahahaha, hell no.

DT/JP: Hahahahahahahahahaha!

KEY TERMS: GATEKEEPER, TRISTAN, LIKE ME, THE DIRTY
Submitted on 12/17/10
Green

After much encouragement from some of my readers (mainly family, but I'll take it) I've decided to try and spread the word about this blog a little more. During my last session with my counselor, I reached two milestones: one, I gave this link to him (welcome to .e4) and two, I believe I finally came to terms with how I want this all to go. He asked me when I will think I've made it. So I told him:

"When I've helped someone, someone like me."

Which sounds good and all, but it's up to me to actually do it. I have always complained that in my greatest time of need, I could find little information anywhere about BMD that I could relate to. "Mood swings," my ass: ask my mom if that's what she calls it when I cry uncontrollably and beg not to hurt anyone. If I am the gatekeeper of my BMD and may have a gift that would help others, then what type of person would I be if I didn't share it? Tis the season.

My first act of business to spread this craziness was to add my blog address to Bing and Google. As I was completing this task, I began to realize that if I am to be successful in this, then everything must come out about my past, even the difficult things. I would like to introduce everyone to Tristan . . .

Tristan is last seen here with his only known accomplice, Boomer (far left). For a crash course on Booms and Trist, here's the story behind the picture. Halloween eve 2004, two young Witt coeds are anxiously awaiting their dates for the movie *Saw*; perfect way to start the Halloween weekend, wouldn't you say? The doorbell rings, and standing outside, grabbing their crotches and mean-mugging to all get out, are Boomer and Tristan. They fill the night with beer, being badass mofos, and "fuckin' partying!"

You could say Tristan is something of an alter ego, but I hadn't heard from him lately, so he was out of sight, out of mind. He used to wreak havoc on my social life in college, randomly appearing at night to offend girls and chase away my hopes of being generally accepted on campus. Damn him, damn him, damn him.

It was a good thing I hadn't seen him or Boomer in a while because like I said, I've been trying to build this blog, and the last thing I needed was those two dicking off. Well, of course I spoke too soon, because there was a Boomer spotting in late summer at the funnel waterslide (they looooove water parks) in Browntown. I shrugged this off and paid little attention, as I was trying to piece my life back together at the time. I recently received an anonymous tip to check out the following link: http://thedirty.com/2010/12/tristan-douchebag/#comments, where I found:

<u>Tristan = Douchebag</u> Posted in <u>Denver</u> | December 15th, 2010

THE DIRTY ARMY: Hey Nik, This d-bag used to date my friend but sent this picture of himself "ballin" right after they broke up to me to try and hook up! He thinks gettin hammered on Arbor Mist is cool and is known to have gonosyphilaherpaids. Please put him on blast for me to warn the ladies of Denver venturing out downtown. BTW, he's wearing shades b/c he got punk'd at the bar by a chick!!!

And he's covering up as much as he can with that sweater to hide his online gamer's body--Nik

I have no idea what he's doing in Denver other than obviously pissing off the local ladies, but I'm beginning to get nervous. I mean, just when I have built up enough confidence in myself to try and do something good, he comes along and starts to ruin it. I'm fairly nervous that if I show my face in Denver ever again, it could get ugly due to mistaken identity. On the brighter side, he's rockin' an .e4 logo hat, so big ups for that one, Tristan. I'm sure I'll be seeing you soon . . .

SESSION

DT: Hey Nik, I don't really like video games because of my mania, so the joke is on you!

JP: You really got him with that one; you don't look like the STD-infested creep on a pathetic wanna-be celebrity website or anything.

DT: Wow, you're definitely right about that. Talk about one of my all-time backfires.

KEY TERMS: SISSY FIT, SABBATICAL, MANIC, ROOF SLIDING
Submitted 1/14/11
Green

"SNAKE!"

I snapped down and grabbed the two-foot-long white stick with black horizontal stripes and tossed it towards Cuzin Art. The mountain striped stick snake hit Cuzin Art's upper leg, and he reacted like a veteran hiker. Screaming (just a little, man, I hate snakes too, cuz), jumping/running in place, and trying with all his might to escape the snake, but not to lose his footing as we were a good ways up the mountain. Still clutching a tree for support, he looked down and realized what had been going on.

"Man, I haven't been scared like that in a while. I thought that snake was going for my sack, man!"

At this point in our hike, I had to sit down and regain my composure. I was laughing so hard at Cuzin Art, I got a little lightheaded. Hey, we were like 9000-plus feet up, and I'm really out of shape. The old inanimate object-throwing at your friend and screaming something scary trick, I can't believe it still works.

If we were good (and when weren't my brothers and I angels?) we would spend about a week every year on vacation with Stubby on the East Coast somewhere. Being the mature and well-adjusted family we are, this meant new territory for us brothers to torment each other. The handful-of-sand-crab trick was a family favorite and the inspiration for the mountain striped stick snake described above. Wading out in the water with my brothers, the object was to bend down nonchalantly and grab a handful of wet sand, slowly bring it to the water's surface, scream "CRAB!" and throw it against your brother's back and enjoy the screaming sissy fit that followed. Watching one of your family members scared out of their minds on your account is just funny, unless of course you're the victim; then everyone else is just a dick.

I've spent the last two weeks on vacation (I know I'm on a sabbatical from life but still, getting away is nice) up in the mountains, Denver . . . gorgeous. This was the first time I had visited the Mile High City since episode uno forced my move back home. I wasn't sure what to expect when I landed there, but I believed I'd find something: maybe closure, maybe a new beginning, maybe peace with it all or maybe just some answers.

My first stop was the toughest-- the house I'd climbed when I was manic. My stomach fluttered as I pulled into the parking lot of the restaurant next to the house. I had forgotten just how tall it was and how steep its roof was. I walked around, looking up and trying to remember how I climbed to the top. I know stairs were not an option, *anyone* can take the stairs and *I* was on mission. The support beam that I swung from, that saved my life or at least some severe injuries, was still there, and I still can't believe how I didn't fall off that roof sliding down it. Somebody up there must like me.

TBC . . .

SESSION

JP: When you climbed this house, just how manic were you?

DT: Well, I'd say I was pretty severe at that point. My memory fades in and out around that time, which is a strong indicator of how gone I was.

JP: Interesting. Did you experience any manic symptoms when you returned to the house?

DT: No, just some nervous butterflies in my stomach. I just kind of stared up at it and tried to imagine what was going on in my head that convinced me climbing it was a good idea.

JP: So why do you think you did it?

DT: When I'm manic, it's as if I don't have much control over what is happening with me, and I'm simply along for the ride. That ride probably took me to that house, and I probably felt like that's where I belonged, on top of that roof.

JP: Just how far would the fall have been? You mentioned the support beam saving your life or the very least serious injuries.

DT: Well, I took some pictures on my phone. Here, have a look. . . I don't know, it looks like about thirty feet high or something. Definitely high enough that I wouldn't ever wanna try a roof slide again, that's for sure.

KEY TERMS: KARMA, "PATIENTS," NOMADIC RENEGADE, SCANTRON
Submitted on 2/4/11
Green

- Three new *Sports Illustrated* (I really don't care much for Rick Reilly now that I can hear his voice)

- *ESPN the Magazine* (why must this magazine always be so much bigger than everything else in the mail?)

- Credit card offer (yeah, that's what I need, credit card debt in my life)

- W-2 (OK, so I used to make this much money in a pay period at AT&Tizzle, makes me feel good about myself)

- U.S. Olympics Team newsletter (they gave me address stickers, with the wrong address but a nice gesture nonetheless)

- Ohio Department of Mental Health survey (they probably picked the wrong random participant)

So come to find out, karma really does exist because as soon as I got my W-2 in the mail and was reminded of how little I do with my life, something good happened to me. Out of tens of thousands of "patients," I was one of like 6,000 randomly selected to participate in this year's survey, to determine just how well the ODMH serviced me last year. Mind you, these are the same people who tried to put me in rehab; outpatient rehab, but damn it, that's still rehab in my eyes. After opening this piece of good news, I could barely contain my excitement as I drove back to the sticks from Mom's. I'm a nomadic renegade who's moved seven times in the last five years, so my mail gets scattered throughout the country. Pain in the ass.

I didn't complete the survey that night. I thought it best to sleep on it. In hindsight, I probably should have slept on it a couple of nights. I didn't rate the ODMH very highly because they literally made my life more difficult to live. I was flying through the fill-in-the- blank scale questions, and I wished that the survey was on the old Scantrons. That way, when they slid my survey through, all they'd hear were those awful signaling clicks. I used to love hearing those clicks in the hall whenever I'd pass the teacher's lounge, always meant someone bombed (oh, like you don't laugh at times at other people's failures). I was answering questions about their administrative performance, parking at the office, ease of finding the office, responsiveness, and how I'm doing as a result of the services provided. Strongly disagree down the board.

The last section was titled:

Please answer the following questions to let us know how you are doing

I was thinking, great, they're going to check on my condition; they hadn't asked about that yet. You know, my age, sex, mental health condition, living conditions, work conditions, social interactions, self-esteem levels, happiness levels, et cetera . . . Wrong. They only asked two questions:

Are you still getting mental health services? (yes)

How long have you received mental health services from your provider?

   a. Less than a year (continue to question 39)

   b. One year or more (continue to question 42)

Questions 39-41 and questions 42-44 were the same. The ODMH only wanted to know if I had been arrested anytime in the previous two years and the occurrences of my encounters with the police over the past year. Even though there was not a space provided for a comment, I let the surveyors know how I felt about those last few questions: "The simple fact you ask about my police record more than my health record is <u>insulting</u>. This is once again a total waste of tax revenue! Instead of focusing on improving this health sector, you would rather investigate mental health relationships with drugs, crime, etc. . . . PATHETIC!!!"

Really glad I waited a day to cool down before completing that survey.

SESSION

JP: If you were so unhappy with the services, why didn't you just get your care elsewhere?

DT: I tried, believe you me, I tried. But with my preexisting condition, I couldn't receive insurance coverage anywhere I looked, so I was basically stuck. My plan was to ride out the summer as best as I could in Chicago and then get healthcare from the job I'd hopefully get from my internship. This would have allowed me to get my much-needed lithium, but that didn't really work out like I planned. That whole preexisting-condition excuse is nonsense if you ask me. I mean, the insurance agents won't even talk to you. Even the secretary knows you're fucked and basically tells you good luck, then hangs up. These are people's lives that are being affected, but I don't think they can see past the profit margins or whatever other financial explanation they have on their business plans.

KEY TERMS: RIGHT HOOK, FIRST LOVES, SOUL, MADNESS
Submitted on 2/25/11
Green

"Why are you down there?"

"Well, Jill, last night on the walk back to the dorm from the bar, you decided to punch me in the face, so I decided to sleep on the floor."

"Ha-ha, no I didn't. I don't remember that."

"Oh yeah, you definitely did it. The people behind us found it pretty entertaining as well. I can't believe the first person to sucker punch me was my girlfriend . . ."

Ah, first loves, they do so much more for us than we realize at the time. I had no idea taking a right hook from my first love could actually pay off in the long run, but it has (well, my dignity is still a little roughed up, but you'll have that). The other day on Sirius (those clever bastards put satellite in my new Jeep so of course I'm addicted now and will have to renew) I heard a song that reminded me of my first girlfriend, Jill, and I'd like to share some of those memories with you now.

I remember when we took our first vacation together in Panama City, and you convinced me to get a tattoo on my lower back. I'm pretty sure you knew the tramp stamp would become the international symbol of sluts within a couple of years, so, um, yeah, in hindsight that was a pretty bitchy move.

I remember when you were too tired to go out on my twenty-first, so we watched a movie and you fell asleep before midnight. So much for getting wrecked (or maybe even laid) like every other person celebrating their twenty-first birthday that night; so, um, yeah, in hindsight that was a pretty bitchy move.

I remember how you never came to the Witt bubble, so I always came "uptown" (there's barely a town in Oxford, let alone the need to differentiate between uptown and downtown) to Miami, so often that when we split, the girls at Witt had never seen me. They assumed I was a freshmen and didn't talk to me for a year, so, um, yeah, in hindsight that was a pretty bitchy move.

I remember when I drove to Miami for your track meet, and then we went out. You gave me a pair of sandals as a random gift, we had sex (you probably faked it, remember admitting that, too?), and then you broke my heart. So, um, yeah, in hindsight that was a pretty bitch move.

I know it sounds like I'm ripping my ex a ton here. But that's not necessarily a bad thing. I realize I'm glad about what happened. If I didn't go through all of that (and more) I wouldn't be anywhere near ready to fight the fight I'm in now. Sure, Jill messed with my head, but what first love doesn't? I needed some of that tough love because what I'm fighting now isn't out to break my heart: it's out to break my spirit and take my soul. So while I may have a Super Sweet Back Tat, a tiny complex in bed, a slight disdain for J. Crew U, and the unsettling fear of a phantom right cross taking me out at any time, they are exactly what I needed. Well, the complex-in-bed thing I could do without, but three out of four ain't bad.

SESSION

JP: First loves do play a significant role in our psyches and emotional states. Did Jill happen to play any role in your mania?

DT: That's the crazy thing; she's never been involved whatsoever. None of my ex-girlfriends play a role in my madness--they did enough of that when we dated. Am I right or am I right? Or am I right? . . . Oooh, you know what I'm talking about.

KEY TERMS: ASH WEDNESDAY, JC, FAITH, PSYCHOSIS
Submitted on 3/18/11
Green

Happy Birthday to Me!
Happy Birthday to Me!
   I'm going to make fun of a religious tradition;
   That's protected under my First Amendment freedom of speech!

I will admit I'm a little behind on Christian traditions from my lack of attending church growing up. I've had docs dig into my psyche about why, and maybe some of it has to do with the fact that the last time I attended church was when Stubby lost his hand. So there might be a link there, but more than likely, I was just a kid who didn't want to go with parents who didn't make me. I never thought this would have affected me until Ash Wednesday at Witt a few years back.

I was working out one day when I kept seeing all these good-looking girls with black smudges on their foreheads. I didn't know if it was some sorority thing, some secret (shhh don't tell) thing, or what, so I went up to one girl and asked what was going on. She said it was for Ash Wednesday, with an arrogant attitude and in that "you're surely going to hell" tone. Oh sorry, I didn't realize you were such a devoted follower of faith, judging from the shots you were slamming and the basketball player you were dry-humping last weekend at the bar. My mistake.

I was so pissed at the exchange that I never even bothered to look up what Ash Wednesday was until this week, when Digger was rocking the ashes on ESPN. I half-assed it at Wikipedia so take it for what it is:

> **Ash Wednesday**, in the calendar of Western Christianity, is the first day of Lent and occurs 46 days before Easter. It is a moveable feast, falling on a different date each year because it is dependent on the date of Easter. It can occur as early as February 4 or as late as March 10.
>
> According to the Canonical gospels of Matthew, Mark and Luke, Jesus spent forty days fasting in the desert before the beginning of his public ministry, during which he endured temptation by Satan. Ash Wednesday marks the beginning of this forty day liturgical period of prayer and fasting.
>
> Ash Wednesday derives its name from the practice of placing ashes on the foreheads of adherents as a sign of mourning and repentance to God. It also means that we will always

have sin. The ashes used are typically gathered
after the palms from the previous year's Palm
Sunday are burned.

This brings me to Lent, which I totally get a kick out of from
time to time. So JC (never even knew he was Jewish till a few
years ago) makes the total sacrifice for forty days and endures
suffering, pain and Satan (not fun, that guy Lucifer sucks at life)
to show his faith. It is impressive. I have trouble finding the connection between that and someone nowadays giving up fast food
for Lent. Which is a real sacrifice and one I couldn't do. I have
an arrangement with the Big Man; I get fast food in return for the
fourteen days of being committed in the wards. But JC roamed
the desert for over a month, battling Lucifer and starvation, and
you gave up a deep fried meal that is free if not accompanied by
a receipt? I feel like someone's getting the better deal here.

I find religion to be fascinating and a vital aspect of society,
but how people practice it just makes me laugh at times. I hadn't
really contemplated my faith until after my episodes (psychosis
will change a man) and for me it's not about the show. It's about
what's inside. So for the 90 percent or so of the people who read
this and are offended, it's my birthday, so give me a break. I've
had a rough few years. I think I deserve it.

SESSION

JP: For those with bipolar disorder, religion often plays a distinct role in their lives. Many find comfort and healing through
prayer and find the support of their church families to be in-
valuable. However, some have also faced misunderstandings,
judgment, and even accusations of demon possession.

DT: I think you should treat others only as you consent to
being treated in the same situation.

JP: That's great, Derek; did you just make that up?

DT: As far as you know.

JP: It's the Golden Rule smart-ass.

KEY TERMS: BIPOLAR THING, BEAKER, TESTS, SIMPLE
Submitted on 3/25/11
Green

"I never would have thought you were bipolar, you don't seem like it."

—Drinking Buddy

I guess we all have our own mental images of what bipolar disorder or any other mental health condition looks like. Before my getaways in the psych wards, I always associated Beaker from the Muppets with mental health. I have no idea why my image is of a Muppet, but I mean, look at Beaker. He's got all the physical attributes of a crazy person. Yeah, that's not considered offensive as long as you're crazy when you say it; it's a bipolar thing. I suppose that I, along with my drinking buddy quoted above, had this preconceived notion of what mental health looks like, as a direct result of the environment we grew up in.

Growing up, I never saw a TV show or movie that portrayed someone with a mental health condition as a real person. They always seemed nonhuman, like they didn't share the same fears, joys, pain or excitement that I felt.

The fact of the matter is that we are real people with real problems, just like everyone else; at least, I hope everyone struggles with online dating as much as I do. We worry about the same life issues everyone else has, except we are given an added burden. No matter what I would have changed or done differently growing up, it would not have affected whether or not I was BMD. Just ask the *M*A*S*H* voices I heard as a child; yeah, we'll get to that not-fully-repressed memory soon enough.

I've been in group therapy and am now in individual therapy. I've had blood work, MRIs, EEGs, and every other complex test out there. Still there is no answer to what my BMD is and where it came from. All of this naturally leads me to wonder: Why do I have this? What am I supposed to do with something that can only be described as craziness? Am I supposed to fight the stigmas associated with BMD? Am I supposed to break the stereotypes my friends and others hold? Am I supposed to be a voice for those who may not be able to speak for themselves? Am I just supposed to write? Can it be that simple?

SESSION

JP: What about Crazy Harry for your Muppet? Look at him!

DT: He looks more like a cracked-out druggie to me.

JP: Yeah, you're right; they probably shouldn't let him have explosives.

DT: It does seem like a dangerous combination for educating the youth.

KEY TERMS: ATROXTHEATROPHOBIA, #TRUESTORY, CRAZINESS, PURE EVIL

Submitted on 4/1/11

Green

So my blood work came back from the lab this week. You would have known about this if you followed my tweets; you really should, I'm funny sometimes. One irregularity popped out at me. They can't tell a lick about my BMD from these tests, but they did find out about my immense fear of scary movies what I call atroxtheatrophobia. My brothers despise them too, so it's a family trait.

I've only gone to the theater and watched three scary movies in my life:

1.) *The Blair Witch Project* in high school with Cuzin Art (I still make him go down basement steps before me).

2.) *Saw* while I was in the Witt Bubble on a double date (well, Tristan and Boomer went, so I had shades on in the theater and kept my eyes closed through most of it; #truestory#fact#honesty).

3.) *A Nightmare on Elm Street* in A-Town with my
girlfriend whose name was so Southern she hy-
phenated it; she was way out of my league, and
she got a kick out of annoying me by getting the
entire ticket line to make fun of how nervous I
was about the scary movie (good thing she was
fine as hell or I wouldn't have put up with that
shit; who am I kidding, yeah, I would).

Ever since I can remember, I've had this fear of scary movies
and shared it with my brothers. I think Monkey put it best when
he described why he hated horror movies: "Let's see how you
do when you're a seven- or eight-year-old kid and you're home
alone, out in the middle of the country in a remote cornfield,
and your older brothers are the only ones around; and they're
scared as hell too. I guarantee you won't be watching any of that
scary movie shit then."

The last thing my brothers and I were about to do on a dark,
cold, weary and eerily calm night in the country was watch *Children of the Corn* (oh, and Crybaby Bridge; not real fond of you
either). Instead, my brothers and I could probably be found
watching Comedy Central and trying to laugh the fear out of
our minds.

So of course when it comes to handing out symptoms of
BMD, I get dealt one of my ultimate fears of horror films: psychosis. What can be more terrifying than the complete unknown?
Nothing scares me like pure evil. Pure evil has no reason, no
cause, and no justification for its ways; how can something without sympathy do anything else? That is what I see in my mania.
It comes as it pleases and does as it pleases. The craziness that
overcomes my world can be described simply as my own person
horror film come to life. Yet I've found pride in living with this.
Pride in knowing I am strong enough to overcome my worst
fears and then some. And I'm proud to know that I live in what
others can only experience in horror movies. Boy, that sounds
crazy, which kind of makes sense.

SESSION

JP: This entry reminds me of an article I read a few years back in the *New York Times* May 11ᵗʰ, 2008 issue by Grabrielle Glasert titled "'Mad Pride' Fights a Stigma", and I want to share a part of it with you because I think you will like it, Derek:

> "Until now, the acceptance of mental illness has pretty much stopped at depression," said Charles Barber, a lecturer in psychiatry at the Yale School of Medicine. "But a newer generation, fueled by the Internet and other sophisticated delivery systems, is saying, 'We deserve to be heard, too.'"
>
> About 5.7 million Americans over 18 have bipolar disorder, which is classified as a mood disorder, according to the National Institute of Mental Health. Another 2.4 million have schizophrenia, which is considered a thought disorder. The small slice of this disparate population who have chosen to share their experiences with the public liken their efforts to those of the gay-rights and similar movements of a generation ago.
>
> Just as gay-rights activists reclaimed the word queer as a badge of honor rather than a slur, these advocates proudly call themselves mad; they say their conditions do not preclude them from productive lives.

JP: I'll take it from that ear-to-ear shit-eating grin on your face that you liked it.

KEY TERMS: "CONTENTED CAMEL," DIFFERENT, LABIA MAJORA, BUTTER
Submitted on 4/8/11
Green

I'm fairly sure all of us are familiar with the classic Hans Christian Andersen fairytale, "The Ugly Duckling." It's a popular tale of redemption for the awkward, unpopular duckling that eventually finds itself and joins the majestic, beautiful swans it was meant to be with. It warms the heart, but unfortunately I can't relate at all. Nope, I'm more like "The Contented Camel." Oh, you've never heard of it? Interesting. Well, I'll break it down then.

The contented camel was very similar to the ugly duckling in that while growing up, he was always different, yet he continued on his own way, just happy to be alive. The other horses would poke fun of his hump ("Humpty Dumpty"), his long eyelashes ("Maybelline called, they want all their mascara back!"), his long neck ("Look at that long neck!"--they weren't very creative with that one) and wide feet ("Cameltoe"). The contented camel went on with his own day, happy to be around and happy to be different: the end; not much of an ending, I know.

I see a lot of myself in the contented camel. I never really fit into the farm crowd; I was a little different from them and always seemed to do my own thing. As I've mentioned, somehow the farm gene skipped me. My brother could spot a tractor a mile out in the field and be able to identify the make, model, year, what it was pulling, and the guy in it by the age of eight. I still pop the trunk to check the oil.

I was friends with this group but not part of it. I played soccer (grass fairy) and ran track while the "jocks" played football and basketball. I wore "queer earrings" instead of Wranglers, smoked a little (just a little) bit of dope instead of putting in a chaw during class, and put out the vibe instead of hanging out in a cabin. I can also relate to the whole nickname shenanigans that the contented camel faced.

It was junior high, and even though the girls didn't have much interest in me, I had tons in them. I was searching for any in with the females. One day, when my crush since like the fifth grade (I fall hard, kids) gave me a nickname, "Butter," I thought I had broken the code; I thought I was in. All the girls were talking to me and calling me every variation of Butter you can imagine. I'd finally made it. The nickname stuck through high school and even spread to some nearby schools, but of course it was all too good to last. Come to find out, I had come to school that day in junior high with really yellow teeth, so that's why I got the nickname "Butter" (woh woh waahh). So I can sympathize with the contented camel's being nicknamed after the outline of a human female's labia majora, sort of.

I guess the point I'm trying to make (if there is one) is that I was always a little different growing up. I don't think it hurt me. I didn't have to take any abuse or anything excessive like that, and I was pretty content with being different; maybe even a little proud of it. Sure, I may not have been cut from the same cloth as many of the kids around me, but I was me, and I'm not sure they can all say that. Maybe it was good I was different and took a little bit of guff for it (it's all in good fun anyhow; except for you Cedarville punks, I still despise you) because now I'm a lot different and only getting more so by the day, it seems. It could have been worse, I suppose; I could have been nicknamed after a woman's genitalia.

SESSION

DT: I probably have to explain what a cameltoe looks like for you, JP.

JP: Nope. Remember, I used to have sex with women before I came out.

DT: That's right. Was it as uncomfortable and awkward for them as it was for you?

JP: More than likely; I really wasn't into it.

DT: Don't worry about it. I'm all in and still can't figure out how to pleasure women. I mean, half the time I just lie there, let her take control and try not to screw anything up.

JP: How's that strategy been working out for you?

DT: Some times better than others.

KEY TERMS: NEPOTISM, OUTPREPARED, AMBITION, STRANGER
Submitted on 4/15/11
Green

"By failing to prepare, you are preparing to fail."
— Benjamin Franklin

I didn't have the professional business skills (hell, someone had to teach me how to fax my first day at AT&Tizzle), the summer internship(s) in college (too busy yelling at Lady Tiger joggers on Fountain Avenue from the seal truck; ♪ "I SEE YOU BABY; shaking that ass, shaking that ass!" ♪), nepotism or networking behind me (unless I wanted to farm, no G'Pa I'm sorry, I still don't), or strong academics with multiple clubs and recognitions (I actually missed the GPA cut-off for ASAP (AT&T Sales Apprenticeship Program, damn, they loved acronymns), so I lied a tiny bit on my resume. Oh, like *you're* perfect. To compensate for all of this, I was determined to not be outworked or outprepared.

Don't get me wrong. There were some days when I would ride the elevator up to work in the mornings and be absolutely miserable. I would doubt myself the whole ride up on why I decided to leave everyone I knew and everything I was comfortable with for getting my butt kicked in at work, day in and day out. I mean, I was a Communication (no "s") major from the cornfields of central Ohio who knew nothing about city life, Southern ways, telecommunications, business etiquette, or office behavior. But I had a plan and knew no one would outwork me to get it.

That plan was simple: take my lumps for three or so years learning the ropes, then go dominate in Silicon Valley. I'm referring, of course, to the lucrative partnership of the porn and telecommunications industries:

(per Family Safe Media: http://www.familysafemedia.com/pornography_statistics.html)

- Every second, $3,075.64 is spent on pornography.

- Every second, 28,258 Internet users are viewing pornography.

- Every second, 372 Internet users are typing adult search terms into search engines.

- Every thirty-nine minutes, a new pornographic video is created in the United States.

I guess I should say thanks for taking a break from your porn addiction to read this. I really appreciate it.

I was working hard and found pride in knowing that I was the farm boy from nowhere, succeeding and making my way up the corporate AT&Tizzle ladder; it was gratifying and made me happy. You'd think those life lessons would pay dividends when fighting my BMD, but it's done the opposite.

At AT&Tizzle, I always had my yearly business plan completed. I had my sales funnel up to date per quarter and sales estimates per month down to the day if possible. My days were scheduled out in my calendar with meetings and notes throughout the hours, and my trusty daily lists of projects to complete could always be found by my side. I remained conscious of my big-picture goal of continued success and upward movement while at AT&Tizzle. I could live with failure but not failure due to my lack of effort. If it was within my control, I saw no reason why I shouldn't be prepared for it. I could accept losing a deal, customer or whatever due to outside circumstances, but it drove me crazy to think of losing due to lack of planning on my end. There was simply no excuse in my mind.

But now with my BMD, the planning and hard work ethic have backfired in a big way (see the past two years of my life). My ambition and drive come back to haunt me by getting me too deep into situations that I'm not ready for (Chicago) and I end up hurting myself more. I'm not good at sitting on my hands and waiting (well, unless I'm giving myself a stranger; yeah, I like porn too) because I feel like I'm failing to prepare and preparing to ultimately fail. But I've got to see the big picture and realize I have to do essentially nothing for a while to make sure I'm alright. I'm just trying not to go crazy doing nothing in order to make something out of my life. It just feels awkward and alien to me, kind of like the first time I watched porn.

SESSION

JP: According to a study in 2000 by Robert Carson, bipolar disorder is typically a recurrent disorder. A significant association between high levels of stress and manic-depressive episodes was revealed, and stress was also an important continuing factor in those who had more episodes. The study found that patients with more prior episodes were more likely to have an episode after a stressful event. I'd say you are doing the correct thing in this entry of waiting it out and avoiding those familiar stressful situations.

DT: Still doesn't change the fact I feel like a bum at times.

KEY TERMS: BRITS, EFFIN' TEA, JOKES, BEING DOWN
Submitted on 4/29/11
Green

Leave it to the Brits to eff up easy things like tea and jokes.

Did you know that there are two tea times, with different types of food and different-sized tables at different locations for each time? There are actually times in the day when they're restricted to drinking tea. I mean, give me a break; it's effin' tea. I love tea when it's simple and easy, ice-cold, sugary and refreshing. Sure, I'll church it up with the sophistication of going halves with some lemonade and calling it a distinguished and respected golfer (Arnold Palmer, that's for my editor who didn't get that reference) but that's where I draw the line.

Same philosophy goes for jokes: simple and easy. Coincidentally, it's the way I like my women too; I kid, I kid. I was watching the special "Talking Funny" a couple of nights back with Jerry Seinfeld, Chris Rock, Louis C. K. and Ricky Gervais on HBO. I stumbled upon it by accident and got really excited because I thought it was an interesting group of comedians, and I was really interested in what they had to say. I regret it now after listening to that effin' tea sippin' Brit, Ricky Gervais.

I admit there were some interesting and hilarious conversations. One in particular revolved around the word nigg—

What's that, conscience? I shouldn't say that word? Not even if I have a picture representin' *I'm Down* (writer Mishna Wolff's memoir; read it, peeps) like this:

**(Myself and Jamin, a college friend of mine known for being "down",
being "down" for Ohio's Bicentennial)**

Still no? Well, OK. The N-word between mainly Rock and C.K. was definitely entertaining, but it was ruined when the subject changed and Ricky started going off on this tangent about the authenticity of a laugh and the elements of different styles of comedy. Told you only the Brits could eff it up. That redcoat was sucking all the fun out of the show. I should note that Seinfeld and Rock seemed like they would agree with me on this; of course, Louis C. K. was just being a pompous ass. Note to reader: Gervais's annoying preschool girl laugh nearly sent me back to University Hospital (Southside!) as well. I felt Ricky was bound and determined to make a joke more complex than it needed to be. He had to overanalyze everything in order to legitimize his jokes and the laughs he was getting. I know, what a dick.

I took offense to this because I try to use humor in the simplest way I can. That usually includes a lot of material about dicks and farts, but I have seen how well it can work. I love how a joke can allow us to discuss sensitive subjects in a nonthreatening manner. I love how laughter can break down preconceived notions about issues by making them real and relatable. I truly love how my comedy in its best and simplest form can help people relate to one another even if the subject is something crazy like BMD. Oh, and don't even get me started on those effin' scones either.

SESSION

DT: Let me hear one of your favorite jokes, JP.

JP: OK. A pirate walks into a bar and the bartender yells, "Hey! You know you got a steering wheel coming out of your crotch?" The pirate responds: "Arrrrrrrrrrrggh, it drives me nuts."

DT: Hahahahahahahahahaha, I love that effin' joke!

KEY TERMS: SEX, "DIFFERENT," COMMITTED, PATIENT CAMARADERIE
Submitted on 5/13/11
Green

A wise man once said:

"Find a girl that loves to have sex, because then once you're married, she'll still actually want to have sex."

I heard this quote just a few months after my first (and kind of pathetically) only girlfriend up to that point decided to trade me in for a newer model. I took the breakup not so well and was looking for solace of some sort. It was the summer of my sophomore year in college, and I had been under the assumption that I was different in some way from my g.f. (and possibly every other woman, though due to my limited exposure I had no proof) because I always wanted to have sex and she rarely did.

So when I heard this piece of golden knowledge above, I decided to test the theory out for myself and hopefully find the solace I was looking for in a physical form. Come to find out that there are a number of young ladies out there who love sex as much as I do: awesome. It felt great to find others who were "different" like me; almost like I wasn't the different one.

Back in Denver, when I first awoke in the Porter Hospital psych ward, I was completely out of it and convinced I had been placed in some kind of governmental hiding/protection program (don't you hate it when that happens?). But after a couple of days, I was able to come out of my delusions and step far enough back into reality to realize that I was committed. I'm not sure how someone is supposed to feel when they come to this realization. Would shame be the appropriate feeling? What about embarrassment? Or maybe even disappointment? Suggestions, anyone?

The weird thing was that I didn't feel any of those feelings and still don't to this day. I felt a kind of calm about the entire situation, like I knew I was meant to be there. I knew, and still know, that those two weeks in the wards will always make me different, even if it doesn't make me feel different. I've contemplated this for a while and have been trying to put my finger on why I was so comfortable there.

I think I figured it out sometime last week when I was cruising around (Jeep wave): the very thing that made me different was what made me the same in there, just like sex did back in the day. My days in the wards (especially in Southside! due to holiday limited staffing) were mostly filled with free time, which to psych ward patients isn't necessarily the best thing. I really didn't need any more time to think. I was all good with my manic racing thoughts as it was. You end up spending the majority of your time with the other patients. I didn't even see my ward's doc in The Nasty until the day before I was released. This lack of attention inevitably leads to patients leaning on each other.

I mean, who else can better understand what hell you have just been through than the ones who are walking alongside you? We only had each other in there to get better, because we were the only ones there who understood how to get back. So maybe it's what made me different outside that made me feel so at home in the wards. What was different was all around me.

SESSION

JP: It seems to me from this entry here, Derek, that you had a strong camaraderie with the other patients in the wards. How exactly did these relationships form?

DT: Well, when I was in the ward in Denver, I had a couple of patients come up to me and just talk some stuff out. It was therapeutic for me to listen, so I followed their lead and reached out to new patients and recognizable ones, too. The bonds started there and just grew for me.

JP: It sounds gratifying, knowing you helped someone else who was suffering like you.

DT: Yep, you nailed it; it's even a little addictive as well.

KEY TERMS: FACEBOOK, DEAR PENTHOUSE, SO GAY, TRUST ISSUES
Submitted on 5/20/11
Green

I was Facebook-stalking the other day (how else am I supposed to efficiently keep track of all my exes?) when I stumbled upon an old photo which instantly made me start cracking up. This wasn't necessarily because of the picture itself, but more the story behind it. First things first, though, have a look at the picture I'm talking about:

(This will all hopefully make sense by the end)

I have no idea how to properly tell this story, so I'm just going to do it by fulfilling a childhood fantasy.

<u>July 2006 Issue</u>
Dear Penthouse,

I never thought I'd be one of those guys writing to you, but I had to share this story. I've been dating this smoking hot Southern belle who is the forward type if you know what I mean (she grabs my junk a lot in public if you didn't). Anyway, one night we get home and she pulls me through my apartment door and into my bedroom. Before I have any time to react, she has my pants unzipped and with the utmost Southern hospitality is saying hello to my junk. Well, of course I take the gentleman's high road and allow her to finish their conversation down there. About halfway through, she starts to laugh; mind you, my junk is in her mouth at this time (awkward to say the least). I asked what the matter was, and she insisted nothing and continued with her conversation. A few moments later, she starts to crack up hysterically once again, so I look down and say:

"What the hell? What's so funny, and don't say nothing. I mean, my dick is in your mouth and you're cracking up; it's starting to give me a damn complex!"

She pauses her conversation and responds:

"You're just standing so gay with your hand on your hip, leg straight out, and head tilted up to the side. Every time I look up, I start laughing."

Needless to say, we finished things up *lying* on the bed, and I'll no longer be trying that standing position any time soon.
Ashamed in Atlanta,
Derek

You can imagine I wasn't really proud of this moment in my life at the time and really didn't want the story to get out. However, I felt it was my moral responsibility to at least tell my best friend, trusting that he wouldn't tell anyone. What is a best friend good for other than to keep vulnerable/embarrassing secrets, right? Apparently, they are also good for spreading the word. The next time I visited Browntown and walked into the bar, the bartenders, bouncers, DJ and even some patrons were all standing "so gay" with their hands on their hips, legs straight out and their heads tilted up (see photo evidence above). It was hilarious, and I definitely have trust issues with my friends, but who doesn't? I mean, they're just looking out for you. You trust them to prevent you from doing that dumb shit again by making fun of you.

I wish I had that type of trust issue with my docs now. Unfortunately, my trust issue with them is simply that I don't believe they have *my* interests at the top of their priority list when we meet. Often, I don't feel like my needs are the ones that the docs are most concerned with. I surely don't expect them to take their work home and dwell on their patients, but a little effort once every six to eight weeks for forty-five minutes shouldn't be too much to ask. I'm probably venting a bit here because I had a real bad meeting last week with the docs. I feel like the new-toy feel has rubbed off of me for the docs, and I'm just another client for them to routinely treat. It can really make me miss my Dear Penthouse days.

SESSION

JP: So how exactly were you standing *so* gay? I think I should be offended, but just show me real quick.

DT: OK, I was standing just like this . . .

JP: Oh, never mind, yeah, that's definitely so gay.

ELEVATED
(YELLOW-ORANGE-RED)

ABSTRACT:

THE ELEVATED SECTION OF THE MOOD CHART ENCOMPASSES THREE LEVELS OF INTENSITY. YELLOW IS THE MILD LEVEL WITHIN ELEVATED MOODS AND IS CHARACTERIZED BY A LACK OF SIGNIFICANT IMPAIRMENT AND THE ABILITY TO WORK. NEXT IS ORANGE, THE MODERATE LEVEL WITHIN ELEVATED MOODS, HIGHLIGHTED BY SIGNIFICANT IMPAIRMENT BUT WITH THE ABILITY TO WORK. THE FINAL LEVEL IS RED, THE MOST SEVERE. IN THIS ELEVATED MOOD, THERE IS SIGNIFICANT IMPAIRMENT AND AN INABILITY TO WORK. THIS SECTION CONSISTS OF THIRTY-SIX ENTRIES, WITH RED CONTAINING THE MOST ENTRIES AT FOURTEEN.

YELLOW

(ELEVATED MILD MOODS WITHOUT
IMPAIRMENT, ABLE TO WORK)

KEY TERMS: MD 20/20, COUNTRY ROADS, HAIKU, MANIC STATES
Submitted on 7/9/09
Yellow

Dearest Liquor,

This is quite possibly the toughest letter I've ever had to write, although I'm pretty sure this is only the second letter I've ever written, minus pen pals. (The previous one was one to Jamie Spears. What was with me and the Spears sisters during my episode? Jeez.) So please hang with me as I make my way through this. First off, I want to say it's me and not you. Now, I know this is such a common excuse to end a relationship, but in this case it's absolutely true . . . You know what? Now that I've thought about that last statement for a minute, I know you deserve the truth and I should be nothing but honest with you. It *is* you and this is all your fault. But don't be too hard on yourself; we did have some good times together.

I can still recall our first date like it was yesterday. I was a young boy looking for adventure and fun, and you came into my life in the form of MD 20/20 (Red Grape, of course) ready to open my eyes to endless pleasures. We spent that first night cruising around the back country roads just holding hands (well, I was holding the bottle, but same difference) and looking at the stars. I should have known that night that this would never work, but it felt so right, even during the final four hours of being passed out in the back of my best friend's car as you wreaked havoc on my system (ahhh, memories). After that night, it seemed like we just took off with no desire to look back. We spent weekends together, and you could always pick me up when I was feeling down. No matter what was going on in my life, it seemed like you were always there to pick me up (and eventually lay me down beside the toilet, but beggars can't be choosers).

Now, while our time together was great, you know what you do to me now. For example, let's take last Sunday and Monday when you sent me into a wild range of manic states. Sure, I heart doing Jäger bombs with the rest of them, and I know you have solid relationships with most of my friends, but I doubt that you send them on the same crazy ride as you do to me the day after. I know I may sound a little bit like a hypocrite because we've talked about how mania can be enjoyable at times, but that's when I'm in control (or as close to control as I can be, please stop judging me). After a night with you, the next day is out of control for me, and I deserve better. I know you're going to be fine and will undoubtedly find someone else real soon to replace me (I'm pretty sure I heard somewhere that at any given time, something ridiculous like around 5 percent of the world's population is drunk) if you haven't already moved on.

Even if this is the fact, I wanted to say thank you for the great times we had together and give you something as token of my appreciation. It is a haiku:

You've shown me beauty
And took it right back away
It was a fun ride

SESSION

DT: "Dearest Liquor, I take it all back. Love, Derek."

JP: That's what I thought, but in moderation, Derek Lee.

DT: Wow, talk about the rainbow calling the upside down pink triangle gay.

JP: Inappropriate.

KEY TERMS: "HARD KNOCKS," KNIGHTS TEMPLAR, BLINK 182, DATING
Submitted on 8/12/09
Yellow

I've been sitting in debate for the past few minutes, trying to decide which life-changing topic I wanted to write about in this entry. The top three in discussion are: my dysfunctional attempts to date since my episode, my first show (concert) since my episode, or my childlike excitement for the *Hard Knocks* season premiere tonight. Seeing how everyone in their right mind is excited for "Hard Knocks: Training Camp with the Cincinnati Bengals" (insert felon joke here) I've decided to concentrate on the other two promising topics. The first we'll meddle in is my feeble attempts at dating.

Not that I was any kind of expert in dating prior to my belief that I was a member of the Knights Templar evading capture from the KGB, but try and imagine explaining that to a girl you're trying to date (that's why I just write about it). When I was first released from the hospital, you could say I was having a little trouble adapting to reality (well, if you call running home from the bar to lie in your closet trouble). So I was wide open to any advice on how to handle this transition, and luckily my friends were there to provide some guidance.

One of my good friends led me to some helpful websites. She also mentioned she had read that when dating, I should wait around six months or so before telling the girl I was BMD (danke for that, BTW). All in all, it seemed like a really good idea. I mean, why bring any more hardships to the relationship until you have to? There's more than enough to try and handle without BMD, considering she's dating me.

The first eight months after my episode, I was in no condition to date or even try to, unless I could find a girl in Browntown who enjoyed my depression and inability to take care of myself. Not many takers; I checked online. Once I was able to pull myself off my parents' couch, I moved down to The Nasty and started living a semi-normal life again; I decided to try and date as well. I met a girl a couple of weeks ago and had a real good time with her. She was the first girl I'd considered trying to date in a while, even though she wasn't blonde; she had dyed it dark, though.

I remembered the six-month timeline advised for people with BMD when dating. This posed a problem because the only way I've figured out how to handle BMD is to be straightforward and honest. I mean, this is a part of me now and plays a significant role in my life. I'm not sure I could hold something like that back for six months. Knowing this, I made the decision that I'd be forthcoming about everything right from the start, but this meant I'd better be pretty confident this girl could handle it. I'm fairly sure casual dating is out the door for me; it feels like there's too much crap to deal with for that.

Long story short, I don't think it would be fair to put this girl through it if I wasn't totally into it. That's right: this eligible bachelor is still on the market. To ease my pain, I'm heading to Blink 182 with the elite from Browntown and tons of teenagers tomorrow (perfect).

Prior to moving to Denver, the state makes you sign a contract stating that you will call all concerts "shows" and that you must attend at least one a month in order to be considered a true Coloradan, Coloradian, Coloradoran, whatever. It's a weird bylaw in their state constitution, kind of like it's illegal in Atlanta to tie a giraffe to a telephone pole or lamppost. I agreed to the terms and was pleasantly surprised by how much I enjoyed calling concerts "shows."

I have a confession to make: the Blink show is actually my second show since being back home. The first was O.A.R., but it was right after my near-manic episode in The Nasty in which I resigned from my job, so I pretty much got sloshed during it. Don't remember the show, therefore it doesn't count. I really don't have much to say about the show, but it seemed like the prior topic was getting a bit too serious, and we can't have that now, can we?

SESSION

JP: Bipolar disorder can become an issue from the very start of a relationship. When you first meet someone you like, it's natural to want to make a good impression. Introducing the fact that you have bipolar disorder may not make for the most auspicious beginning. There is always the fear that you might scare the person off and lose the opportunity to get to know one another. At some point, though, you will need to let your partner know that you are bipolar.

DT: Good luck and Godspeed, singles."

KEY TERMS: MUSIC, "UNIVERSAL LANGUAGE," HENDRIX, HALLUCINATIONS
Submitted on 9/2/09
Yellow

I've slowly became addicted to a new channel on my cable service, known simply as the Science Channel. I am totally fascinated by the discoveries, theories and observations that people can come up with; for instance, the whole multiple dimensions and parallel universe ideas going on right now are re-dunk-u-luss (yeah, I said it, re-dunk-u-luss). My intelligence is way, way, way too underdeveloped for me to even imagine debating the theories previously mentioned, but there's another one I'd like to take a shot at: the whole "Universal Language" talk that's going on.

For the sake of argument (plus, I'm not sure if I'm supposed to use MLA, APA or Chicago style to cite a source in a blog) we'll go ahead and assume that mathematics is the Universal Language. The supporters of this so-called theory would more than likely present the fact that numbers do not lie and that everyone in the world agrees on the principles, rules, formulas and equations of mathematics. I am not trying to debate any of these facts, but I will be a brat here and ask:

"What about music?"

Call me old-fashioned, but I believe the term "universal" should be defined as all- encompassing--in other words, every person on earth should be able to communicate using the Universal Language. I for one cannot imagine that all of the 6.7 billion people on this planet understand mathematics. But I would bet my prized Sean Casey (The Mayor) autographed baseball card that all of them can relate to some kind of music.

That is what I consider the amazing thing about music; it speaks to all of us in one manner or another. I do not have a lick of musical talent in my bones; I can't read, play, write or sing along to music, although it should be noted that I could jam on a mean recorder back in my middle school days. However, there's something unbelievable about music that no math problem could ever do to me: send me back to another time in my life.

I love it when I hear a song on the radio or wherever else and I am instantly thrown back to the time in my life when that song was most prevalent. "Jump" by Van Halen came on the other day, and I was immediately transported back to my dad's Ford "Rescue" Ranger in the mid-eighties with the windows down and the music up. My two brothers and I would all be standing up in the back half cab of the truck, just jamming out to those hair band Van Halen classics as we cruised around the back roads of Clark, Greene and Madison counties. Mind you, we were around the ages of three, five, and seven; sorry, Mom, you had no chance with us. I think everyone reading this is thinking of one of those songs that were so popular when they were growing up; so I dare you to go download it now and play it. The images, emotions and utter delight that rush back to you kick the crap out of logarithms.

During my episode last year, I had one of these musical experiences; however, the outcome and overall play out was a bit different. It started with me sitting in my living room listening to music, when all of a sudden the urge to spark a J hit me (that's marijuana in case my hip lingo left you behind). At this point in my episode, I was smoking from time to time to try and calm down from the mania, so that wasn't the unusual part. It was that I was smoking with Jimi Hendrix. There are a few difficult things to explain about this.

One: Jimi Hendrix is dead.

Two: I don't know how to roll a joint.

Three: **Jimi Hendrix is dead**.

How I rolled that joint, I couldn't tell you. Why Jimi Hendrix was there, I couldn't tell you. How Jimi Hendrix was there, I couldn't tell you. I can only come up with a few similarities between us. Jimi Hendrix was twenty-seven when he died; I was twenty-seven at the time of my suicidal thoughts. Jimi Hendrix was BMD; I'm BMD. Jimi Hendrix loved music; I love music. These three things seem so simple, and I think that's the point. I continually make things out to be more complex than they really are or have to be. Life is simple, and I need to try and remember that and live it for what it is. The Universal Language isn't complex math problems to me. It's the freedom of self-expression, and what better form than music: something everyone can relate to.

SESSION

DT: I think we need to be in the right state of mind for this session . . .

JP: Hack, cough, cough, hack, harrumph! So, um, what you are trying to say here is that Jimi is the music.

DT: Hahaha, what? Wow, I remember my first contact buzz.

JP: Whatever, play some Jimi and stop being such a buzz kill.

KEY TERMS: BED-E-BYE, WHITE CASTLE, ADVANCE, PET PEEVE
Submitted on 9/22/09
Yellow

What lies before me is undoubtedly a daunting task, but I had decent sleep last night (I was only woken up about three or four times by crazy dreams involving me quoting movies that don't exist; weird, I know) and feel that I am up to the challenge. Never before attempted on this blog, I am going for a world record (false) by connecting White Castle Chicken Rings (amazing, BTW), the fact that the world is said to be truly flat, advancement in corporate America, and my IQ of 164 (well, that number is highly debatable, but what else can you expect from an iPhone app) all in one entry.

My usual daily bed-e-bye routine (yes, I still call it that, pathetic, I know) consists of surfing through my iPhone apps to catch up on the news and to entertain me during breaks in football. Last night, I downloaded an IQ test and was completely astonished to find out that while I could only interpret two of the eight or so questions, I scored a 164. I'm a good guesser. Now, the previous night during this routine, the fast food craving instantly hit me as I was perusing the Street (that's what I call the *Wall Street Journal* to make it hip) and the only thing I could think of was White Castle Chicken Rings. I skipped (OK, walked, but my excitement was still evident) down to my car and made my way across the river to the deliciousness awaiting me in circular form.

While waiting for my turn, to be as polite as possible to the intercom and thereby the employee speaking to me from it (pet peeve: people who get upset and yell at fast food employees; come on, you're at an establishment that prides itself on serving you hot food in less than three minutes, what do you expect?) I noticed on their menu board that you can order in advance. I actually laughed aloud at the mere concept that we as a society are so fixated on going and going and going that we have to order fast food in advance. I'm still in awe of it right now.

I'm not passing judgment without consideration here, as I was once part of this mass of common thought that if you're not moving up, you're dying off. I was a loyal follower of corporate America's philosophy of advancement at all costs for the betterment of you and the company. It's definitely difficult to not get caught up in this whirlwind train of thought. I mean, who doesn't want to better themselves, who doesn't want to make the most of their life, who doesn't want to make a lot of money, who doesn't want to succeed? But at what price?

I know I fell victim to the belief that if I was not advancing, I was missing out on something better down the road. If I didn't order my chicken rings in advance, I might be a minute late for my meeting, which would cause my boss to give my promotion to my team member who ordered food in. But a weird thing happened after my episode: I woke up. I'm not trapped in a dream bubble (I also got out of the Witt bubble a few years ago, I think) and am ignoring the idea that in order to succeed, you must always be advancing. I'm asking: why does it take top priority and why does it have to be right now? I feel like we're missing out on something.

This approach troubles me when dealing with the medical staffs I've encountered since my diagnosis. The whole time I was being treated, it seemed like the priority was to get me to the next stage. Get me to their ideal comfort level or something. I felt we were always pushing to advance my treatment without taking account of what was really happening. And what if we were missing something because of what we knew to be true from past experiences and diagnoses? What's wrong with slowing down for a second to try to become aware of what's going on, to better understand it?

Why must we rush through life always trying to advance ourselves rather than being grateful for what we have? Who knows, we might even learn something. I mean, we knew it to be true 1600 years ago that the earth was flat. We knew it to be true 450 years ago that the earth was the center of the universe. We knew it to be true 145 years ago that slavery was acceptable in our society. We knew it to be true ninety-five years ago that women should not have the right to vote. We knew it to be true twenty years ago that I couldn't share this with the world by a simple click of the mouse. What do we know to be true today? (Success on achieving the world record, I think, but I've got a call in with Guinness, checking on it now.)

SESSION

JP: You have this labeled as a mild elevated mood in the yellow category. I find that interesting, since I do not see much mania influence. Can you fill me in?

DT: Well, the way I see it, the only way someone can be craving White Castles is if they're fucked up, so I figured my mania has to be playing some role in this one. Kind of like when you were DayWasted last Saturday and made me go get you a ten sack.

JP: I only ate like five.

KEY TERMS: "GUITAR HERO," CRAZY, WOODERSON, REVELATION
Submitted on 11/6/09
Yellow

With Christmas right around the corner, I have made a point of trying to start my shopping list. Please do not be too impressed with this as it simply involves looking at storefront windows as I walk down to Jimmy John's in The Nasty to grab lunch (Country Club = Legit). The other day, I was making this weekly jaunt when I spotted a shirt in a window that caught me a little by surprise; not as surprising as learning that the video game "Guitar Hero" wasn't the pulse of the world, but that's another manic story for later. The shirt read:

"Crazy Bi-Polar Bitch"

At first glance, I really didn't notice the shirt; however, when I tried to look away from the storefront, the rhinestones on the lettering glimmered just so and caught my eye. I was taken aback at first by the shirt and was almost a little offended. I couldn't comprehend how or when bipolar became trendy, although I *am* getting older and maybe losing touch with the youth. This slightly miffed feeling quickly left and I kind of laughed to myself. Not to say my Porter Hospital psych ward stay was funny, but there is some humor to be found in the fact that the only rule there was not to cross the purple line in the carpet, and I had to be repeatedly reminded of this rule. I couldn't keep away from it. It was like trying to eat just one Lay's potato chip. Good luck.

I can remember when I first came home, the word "crazy" struck a nerve in me. I had no problem with anyone knowing or learning that I had had a manic episode and had been diagnosed with BMD, but whenever the word crazy popped into a conversation, I became incredibly defensive. This was ironic because until the episode, I had prided myself on being the crazy one. I enjoyed being the guy everyone believed was crazy because I naturally aligned crazy with fun. I believed that being called crazy was a compliment and something I could be proud of.

Once I moved back home after the episode, the word crazy took on a whole new meaning in my life. Now, I got upset whenever an instance arose--when, say, Stubby would introduce me like this:

"This is my oldest, Derek, you know his brothers, Devon and Denver; and *he's* the crazy one."

There was no harm meant by this, and prior to my episode, I would have loved this introduction. I would have thought that if you believed my brothers were a good time, you figured you would have a blast hanging around with me. However, after a hallucination that Wooderson from *Dazed and Confused* was talking to me during the movie as a symbolic messenger of truth, being called crazy hit a sensitive spot.

I allowed this to go on for a bit and can recall one day after such an introduction, telling Dad that I wasn't crazy and asking him to stop saying that. I thought once I got this off my chest, I would feel a ton better. I was wrong. I had forgotten that I'm not in this alone by any stretch of the imagination.

I forgot that my family and friends are right there alongside me, fighting just as hard, trying to handle my BMD in their own ways. When I saw how much it hurt my dad to realize that saying crazy really bothered me, I had a revelation. What kind of selfish person would I be if I tried to tell everyone involved in this how to act and to handle this BMD?

One of my biggest complaints with my doctors was that they didn't understand what had happened and therefore couldn't help. I was doing the same thing to my family and friends. I have no idea what they are going through and can't understand it, but the difference is they aren't going anywhere. I know I'm a little bit crazy and I forgot how proud I am of that. If I can't handle a little joke with my dad, then this is going to be a long and lonely ride. Oh, and if anyone is looking for a gift on my behalf this holiday season, a "Crazy Bi-Polar Bitch" shirt wouldn't necessarily be a bad idea.

SESSION

JP: I found a study by DBSA that focused on stigmas associated with mental illness. I think it's pretty interesting:

> DBSA commissioned a survey of 1,200 American adults, a sample representative of the U.S. population in terms of gender, race, ethnicity, geography and education, and found that many people still need to be educated about mood disorders, especially bipolar disorder. Stigmatizing attitudes were not held by the majority of people surveyed. However approximately one in four people, which is one in four people too many, believed people with mood

disorders are not just like everyone else (18%); they should not have children (19%); they are easy to identify in the workplace (26%); and they do not live "normal" lives when treated (29%). Two-thirds of survey respondents also held the incorrect belief that mood disorder medications are habit forming.

DT: Well, when you're right, you're right, JP; that is damn interesting. Especially since I would have figured the numbers would have been much higher and therefore a lot worse than these stats show. So that's what I'm talking about, America! I take back all those bad things I said about you behind your back.

KEY TERMS: NICKNAME, THICK SKIN, PSYCHOTIC, NONHUMAN
Submitted on 12/1/09
Yellow

Boney Ass, Scrawny, Skinny, Chicken Legs, Dope Fein Derek, Twig, Grass Fairy, Skin-and-Bones, Butter, Butta, and the list goes on and on.

I am absolutely positive I am not the only one in the world who has been called a nickname from time to time, as it's undoubtedly a rite of passage while growing up. At times these names can be embarrassing or a little bit hurtful but I believe it's all just part of the game. Everyone is going to be made fun of, and name-calling is as much a part of our culture as deep- frying anything and covering it with sugar is. I am by no means unfamiliar with this activity. I have many times in the past dropped a nickname on some totally unsuspecting soul to get a rise out of everyone else around. While my intentions were not always of the best nature, I hope that each receiver of a nickname has a sense of humor and can let it go (and if not, then you deserved it).

I have learned that in order to survive, I must have thick skin. The list of names I've been called and have heard others called is downright impressive and a bit worrisome. To think how much time and effort someone would take to rhyme a name with a non-hygienic body part . . . I'm a little worried of what they could do if that energy was spent elsewhere. But I am not here to change the ways of the youth (hell, I'm no more mature than them, anyway). That being said, I did read my papers from my mini vacation at Porter Hospital psych ward last year, and being called psychotic isn't the best feeling.

I recently sifted through the belongings bag that I was allowed to bring home from Porter Hospital after my episode, and I found a few interesting things. There was the drawing in which I compare myself to an otter (I'm not even sure what exactly an otter is), the short story of my high school buddies and I waking up on a plantation during the Great Depression (not random at all), and my emotions diary which consisted of a business plan for a roller-shoe paintball abandoned warehouse game (all rights and trademarks reserved by .e4). While all of these were interesting, the doctor evaluation that labeled me psychotic was my main focus.

To think I was in a state of mind that caused me to behave in such a way that others feared me--it's something I have trouble grasping. I still think of myself as a five-foot- nothing freshman, walking into high school with a bowl cut and weighing 100 pounds soaking wet; so to try and imagine someone feeling threatened by me is mindboggling. Having this label thrust upon you, implying that you are unstable and a threat to others, takes just about everything you know about yourself and throws it out the window. You feel nonhuman.

I'm not 100 percent sure how I was supposed to take the news, that a professional feared me enough to have me courtordered to be held in a psych ward. But to strip away my identity to the point that I don't feel human probably isn't the result they were looking for. The only way I know how to try and handle it is to pick myself up and keep going. To say I don't care or that I don't think about the names some people might use to describe the bipolar me would be a lie. But it's those name-calling actions as a boy and the ones I still hear today that motivate me to prove them all wrong. This bowl-haired psychotic chicken- legged grass fairy can thank those nicknames for making me who I am today, even if it took twenty-eight years to figure out who that is.

SESSION

DT: It's really ironic, how sure I am of myself here and how in less than a month, I'd be in my second psych ward with psychosis, trying to find myself once again.

JP: The only constant in this universe is change.

<u>KEY TERMS:</u> SOUTHSIDE!, LOST, CHICKEN STOMP, SIS
Submitted on 2/23/10
Yellow

I have a midterm tomorrow in Sports Finance (yes, it's as fun as it sounds) and I have yet to start studying. I really intended to begin last night, but I found a Warren Miller movie on Netflix on Demand, and I spent the next eighty minutes getting lost in my mind. When I was being admitted in The Nasty, the only evaluation question I can remember was:

"What can we help you with while you are here, what do you want from us?"

"I'm lost. I need help getting back."

The next questions they asked, I have no idea about because that first night, all I can recall is sitting in the hallway of the unit (Southside!) rocking back and forth and being absolutely terrified of showering. I didn't want to rinse away the poison and hurt other people; typical bathing issue, ya know.

Luckily, I felt like I was back from being lost about two weeks ago, when I stood up and danced to Pretty Lights' "After Midnight LIVE Mix" by myself in the middle of the day. The following weekend, I attended the farm show in Louisville, Kentucky and had a blast for three solid road trip reasons:

1.) A good road trip will introduce at least one new band/musician/entertainer/stripper into your life. (Rob Heiliger is all of the above and then some)

2.) Quality road trips extend your branches or strengthen your roots. (The Farm Show, Zanzabar, and Chicken Stomp represented this very nicely)

3.) Finally this road trip helped me learn something new about someone. (Cuzin Art is a DICK!!!!!!!!!!!!!!)

The last couple of weeks, I've felt like myself again, which was amazing but unfortunately temporary. I've been feeling my mania again for the first time since the episode. I'm not manic (calm down, Mom). I can just feel it like I did after my first episode, and it can at times pull me places. For instance, I was dead sure I was moving to Chi-Town after my classes for an internship, but lately I've been thinking of a couple of other destinations as well. Now, while the mania may push and pull me from time to time, there's a crazy thing happening: I feel more like myself when I jump from idea to idea than if I concentrate on one thing at a time. Makes perfect sense, I know.

Another reason for my procrastination is that my sis is coming in on Thursday. My sis is a Southern belle of a pony who is currently somehow responsible for the entire city of Atlanta's social calendar; plus she's a newlywed, so her schedule is intense. I almost begin to shake, thinking of her coming to town, because without her I'm not sure where I'd be today.

During episode deuce, the mania really flipped everything on me, and it made me trust absolutely no one, not even myself; weird, I know. So when I needed help, it got complicated to ask for help while at the same time trying to fool myself into thinking I wasn't getting help. This involved like a six-hour conversation on the phone with my sis as I drifted in and out of the levels of consciousness in my mind, holding my breath, crawling on my stomach, flipping my phone, speaking quickly and sharply, and trying not to end mankind . . . just one of those days. Thanks to that lil' pony, I was able to make it to the hospital and ask for help, so the midterm just isn't a priority right meow.

SESSION

JP: Having a strong support system can be the difference between life and death for many people. This group of family members, friends, professionals, and the like can provide a solid foundation for fighting bipolar disorder. It seems here your sister would fit into this group quite nicely.

DT: Yeah, she's unbelievable. To stay on the phone with me and find the hospital and set everything up to make sure I was alright is more than anything I could have ever asked for. I owe her a lot. I've seen people turn their backs on me, and I'd never have thought that was possible, but in the same breath, I've got people like Jenny who would move the earth so I could walk easier. Without my support system, I wouldn't be here today.

JP: Which also means you never would have met me, so lucky you.

DT: Yeah, unlucky in love but lucky in finding middle-aged gay men to share the most intimate details about my life. That worked out quite nicely for me.

KEY TERMS: Why?
Submitted on 3/29/10
Yellow

Why?

Will you please tell me a few things to help me sleep through the night?

Will you please tell me a story that shuts out the darkness and reveals the light?

Does anyone know what it's like to be higher than life?

Does anyone know how to tell the difference between wrong and right?

Have you felt the aftereffects of the notion of righteousness?

Have you felt the satanic whisper in your ear, guiding your life into complete distress?

I can't try to begin to understand what goes on inside my own mind.

I can't try to begin to comprehend the one question I have, why?

SESSION

JP: I really like this, Derek. Color me impressed.
DT: Danke.

KEY TERMS: IT'S SUPPOSED TO LOOK LIKE THAT
Submitted on 7/21/10
Yellow

.i am constantly aksed the same question whenever someone learns of my disordeR .they always seam to desire to no what exactly its likE ?after I tell that i suffer from severe manic episodes witch feature hallucinations, delusional thoughts, and schizophrenic symptoms they ask; what's that likE ?at first I tried to explain it to them in medical terminologY .i would discuss how the brain has chemical reactions and the episodes are somehow connectected to these chemical reactionS .of corse this really didn't shed any lite on the subject so i decided to try and get a little more in deptH .I wood start out by describing what first starts to happen to me physicallY .my hands and arms first begin to tingle and become red and sore (knot exactly like but close enough to lead my mind into believing I have signs of stigmatA) .next a sensation that can only be compared to orgasmic travels up my spine and down my legS .my surroundings begin to take form, not physical form but a feeling of connection overtakes me with theM .time and space become one in front of me and it feels as though i am at the center of it alL .as if everything before me was put there deliberately to serve this purpose at this moment for me to understanD .this euphoric feeling intensifies and thoughts of grandiosity begin shooting intwo my mind at a pace that throws my world in a spiN .i know that it all cannot be true but my perception of reality becomes fogged by the sheer enjoyment of understanding the true meaning of everythinG .at about this point in time (or actually in "timeless-ness", as this aspect has set in and i become trapped between reality and fantasy where time seemingly stops) i begin to see the purpose of this all and become aware that this is not about me, but rather about what I'm trying to bE .there is undoubt-edly good and evil in the world and each is just as powerful as the otheR .i become obsessed with this struggle inside myself and am determined to out play the others set out to bring harm to the worlD .i am being tested to reveal my true character and define the type of man i am, compared to the person I believe myself to bE .this game continues on and my episode intensi-fies as I get lost in my mind and fantasy becomes reality where reality fails to answer the questions continuing to pile up in my heaD .i spend hours into days fighting against myself to under-stand what is happening and debating if the impossible is reaL .voices call to me, the world begins to pass by in harmony, emo-tions become blurred with desires, and my eyes become liarS .the very thought that i understand the system convinces myself I have thrown off the balance and this will inevitably be the rea-son my world collapses onto me, so i sit completely stilL .terri-fied to breath and mortified to think a thought that might be my lasT .it gets to the point where reality and fantasy become so similar and meshed that deciphering which is which becomes nearly impossiblE .I know there's something not quite right going on but just enough makes sense that i continue on falling deeper and deeper into maniA .it becomes as if I am reading something that doesn't look or seam quite right but am still able to understand the meaninG .i become amazed on how it works and push myself to the point that I lose where i started and where I am suppose to gO

SESSION

JP: Bipolar disorder can be linked with sharpened and un-usually creative thinking. The link between bipolar disorder and creativity is widely accepted as fact. When psychologists measure the creativity of those who suffer from bipolar disorder, they are apt to find levels of creative genius that are extremely rare among the general population. Many famous poets, writers, composers and artists were afflicted with bipolar disorder. I'd say there's some creativity involved in this entry.

DT: Yeah, it's become one of my favorites. I think it illustrates the madness of mania perfectly through symbolic use of format, punctuation, grammar and language, imperfect yet seemingly logical. I'm not going to lie; I impress the shit out of myself sometimes.

JP: And we can check off self-confidence from the list of personality characteristics as well.

KEY TERMS: HIDE-AND-SEEK, HATERS, HECKLER, MISSING PERSON
Submitted on 8/31/10
Yellow

As a kid, I prided myself on my ability to dominate at hide-and-go-seek. I was always a little quicker than everyone else, which played huge in my seeking skills, and my slender and agile body type (some may know it as chicken legs syndrome) allowed for great hides. My aunt nearly reported me as a missing person during one game; yeah, I was that good. I decided to try a little hide-and-seek game with my mania, through which I've learned you can't hide from fate, especially when it's Jay Cutler--remember, my archnemesis?

As some of you may recall, I've had my run-ins with Jay in the past, and we've had our differences. Well, I hadn't put much thought to old Jay lately due to moving back home (and then out to the country), trying to find insurance (finally did, thank you very little), and trying to figure out my next steps (I struck out on my Blue Jackets internship [haters] so on to the next). But that all changed this past Sunday.

As is common knowledge, all Sundays immediately follow Saturday nights, so my story begins (with a coincidence I just noticed, weird) at the ballpark with the Reds versus the Chicago Chubs this past Saturday. This was my first experience in the Diamond seats; all you can eat and drink, real nice place. I almost made it fifteen feet into the door before heckling a Chubs fan (her quick-witted rebuttal to my heckling was, "Ooohhh whatever!" . . . point, Derek) and then settled nicely into a few beers. The rest of the night was filled with reminiscing and then forgetting what I was reminiscing about. Oh, what sweet almost-memories. The next day, I woke up and found that a cat had shit in my mouth--not literally, but it tasted a lot like it. Please don't ask me how I know that.

Since I'm now living out in the sticks with Stubby, I had to hightail it home in time to watch (or sleep through) the Reds game. I think I'm going to enjoy living out in the sticks for a while. I mean, nothing else has worked, so why not try this? I've got a lot more space out here, and it's peaceful, probably two things that couldn't hurt me right about meow. I'm having some childhood memories come back to me, from G'ma's raspberry pies to trying not to lose a finger in the planter with G'pa. I think this place is a good stepping stone to whatever may lie next for me. The only issue is, we are so far out in the boondocks that I haven't found Internet service yet. This means I have to come to Browntown to jump online, which is not exactly convenient.

So without the World Wide Web (still don't know why people don't use that term more often, it's kind of fun to say) it was a little difficult to draft my fantasy football team. My team name is Cap'n Geech, but Shrimp Shack Shooters wouldn't fit; close enough. Luckily, the worldwide leader in sports also has auto draft, so I let fate run its course. But please let the record show that I moved away from Chicago and let Jay have the town without a fight. That's just the type of guy I am. I packed up and moved out to South Solon (my road doesn't even have lines, for God's sake) to get away from it all and find myself.

What does fate do to me after my attempts to play nice? It goes ahead and drafts Jay Cutler as my fantasy football quarterback. What a bitch.

SESSION

DT: . . . ninety-eight, ninety-nine, 100. Ready or not, here I come!

JP: I told you at one I wasn't playing.

DT: I'd be scared too if I was you, I would dominate you in some hide-and-go-seek, JP!

JP: Safe! I just touched base.

DT: Very clever, old man. One, two, three . . .

KEY TERMS: DEMIGODS, SPANKY, CLUB PSYCH WARD, FAITH
Submitted on 9/16/10
Yellow

"Feelings of oneness with the entire universe. Visions and images of distant times and places. Sensations of vibrant currents of energy coursing through the body, accompanied by spasms of violent trembling. Visions of deities, demigods, and demons. Vivid flashes of light and rainbow colors. Fears of impending insanity, even death" (Grof, 1989, *Spiritual Emergency*).

This is the opening paragraph to a book I read last summer (don't act like you're not impressed). I suppose I was searching for an explanation of what BMD was, and that was the closest thing I could find. I had just quit my second job in as many years due to my mania, and I was completely confused. I just wanted to know what this was.

I spent hours online googling and reading any site I could on the subject of BMD (maybe Redtube sneaked in there every once in a while). Random, but I also wasted like an hour watching some dude on MySpace named Bipolar Man; wacky stuff. All of the medical sites were too general to even attempt to be helpful, and too sugarcoated for my liking. Their definitions and lists of symptoms for BMD sounded very similar to a veterinarian's description of a kitten's behavior to me.

I was frustrated because I couldn't tell whether what I experienced was so rare that no information existed, or people weren't being honest. The more I get involved with BMD in all its facets, the more I'm beginning to believe that I'm not out of the ordinary, that there are others out there who have experienced similar episodes, but for some reason either-aren't talking or aren't being heard. I'm beginning to think that the reality of BMD is hidden away by the gatekeepers for their benefit. It's difficult to talk about one's weaknesses and troubles, especially when they involve mental health issues, but I can't buy that as an excuse.

During my last getaway at Club Psych Ward (Southside!) I met a mother and daughter who truly inspired me. The daughter was in the unit with me and was fighting her own battles and demons, yet when she spoke of her mother, there was something that lifted her. During groups, she told stories about the troubles her family and especially her mother had been faced with, daily challenges that I have difficulty comprehending. You'd think they'd be broken, without hope. But I met her mother the day I was released, and I'll never forget the few minutes we shared.

She had just been released from the hospital that day after battling an illness, yet she was still there for her daughter. She struggled to stand up as we were introduced, due to having only one arm and one leg. She smiled at me and we chatted for a few minutes. I was astounded at her will and strength and overcome by her outlook in life. These two women who have every reason in the world to hide from the truth and abandon hope are actually lifting me up. As we said our goodbyes, the mother said something I keep with me to this day:

"Keep faith."

TBC . . .

SESSION

JP: Where faith fits in with bipolar disorder is a subject of high interest for me. Many people who are not Christians still believe that they are "good people" and will tell you that they "have faith." To them, it has nothing to do with traditional Christian beliefs, miracle cures, or a Supreme Being. They may say something like, "I just have faith that everything will turn out all right." This is more of a "positive attitude" type of faith and, Christian or not, a positive attitude is very helpful for someone who has bipolar disorder. At the very least, it will help them in their battle against depression. It will also be helpful in managing their bipolar disorder in general.

DT: Couldn't agree with you more, JP. Look at you, on point today and makin' shit happen!

KEY TERMS: BOWL CUT, FIVE, DIARRHEA, TRUST
Submitted on 9/27/10
Yellow

High top
Mullet
Z's on the side
Shirtless
Osh Gosh B'Gosh Bibs
Cowboy Boots

If you got halfway down this list and instantly pictured me as a young boy, I am more than a little concerned (aside from you, of course, Mom). But that is exactly the look I used to rock back in the eighties. Dead sexy, I know. Over the years, my hairstyle decisions didn't get much better. Being the grass fairy I was, I had the bowl cut get slipped in somewhere in the early nineties, and it persisted into high school. I would make tiny alterations to my bowl, which included shaving underneath and putting my number shaved in the back (can't believe I had my V-Card into my late teens).

My number growing up was five, and I had no idea why I chose that number until now. I think it was an omen of some kind to tell my future self (present-day me) that the fifth doctor I see will be the last. It's a stretch but does give me some hope.

Since I was able to find insurance, I've been on the hunt for a new doc. The UC doc (El Doc) was great but doesn't have a private practice, so it was back to the hunt. I'll admit that I'm not the most cooperative patient due to trust issues I've had so far with my docs. The first doc I was sent to in Colorado after I was released from Club Psych Ward Porter Hospital was easy to find. This was probably due to the fact that the doc's office was in the Kaiser Permanente building in Denver. Wait a tick, Kaiser Permanente was my insurance company at AT&Tizzle (yeah, I don't see a possible conflict of interest or anything).

I will also say the next couple of docs were real pieces of work. My first and last appointment with one doc involved the following closing arguments from yours truly:

"YOU CAN TAKE YOUR RESEARCH AND THROW IT OUT THE FUCKIN' WINDOW BECAUSE WHEN I'M MANIC THE ONLY THING THAT MATTERS IS GETTING BACK!"

I do like my new doc, but there is one little annoyance--OK, two: she calls BMD my illness, not a fan of that; and she wants me to take another medicine to help level me out. I told her I'd do the research on it and let her know, but I highly doubt I'll add anything. I feel my lithium is working and my side effects are nearly gone, save the occasional instance when I'm sliding into third and feel a little turd, diarrhea (that reminds me, the Red-legs' magic number is one; got my playoff tickets, look for me to rebut Colin Cowherd's ridiculous Reds rants of regularity--alliteration is fun).

This is the fifth doc I've seen. If I stick with her, that would make the soccer-number-shaved-in-my-head prophecy come true, but it's difficult to trust someone who wants to medicate you more after spending only twenty minutes with you. All I hear about is trying to level me out. What's good about that? This BMD is all over the place, and being numbed into a level at which someone *else* feels comfortable is not living. I'm not going to do it again.

SESSION

JP: What research was the doctor referring to that got you so fired up?

DT: Well, it was an outpatient rehab program, and this was my initial meeting, which was arranged through the State due to my lack of insurance and apparently poor evaluation. He was describing some study about how substance abuse has been found in research to lead to mania or mania-like symptoms. It was at the point where the culmination of all the frustrations I had been dealing with after my second episode blew up, and I lost it.

JP: It happens to the best of us.

KEY TERMS: DICTATE ME, .15 PERCENT, LIGHTNING BOLT, DEFINE ME
Submitted on 6/3/11
Yellow

I never wanted BMD to define me, to dictate what moves I may take in life, or to change me. I think for that reason, I refused to read or research anything about BMD the first eight months or so after episode uno and my official bipolar disorder type I diagnosis. I suppose at the time I figured if I didn't know anything about BMD and its effects on its sufferers, then I couldn't change, and therefore BMD wouldn't be able to dictate my life or define me. A feeble attempt to try and stop the inevitable, I suppose.

Two years ago this coming week, I started writing this blog as a form of therapeutic release, a way to tell my family and friends what was really going on in this crazy head of mine, and maybe as a way to share the craziness in my life for the world to hopefully enjoy. Over the past two years, I've seen not only myself but my blog change because of BMD, and I believe it's for the better. I came to this conclusion with the following statistical support from random bipolar websites (don't act like you're not impressed, but if you doubt me check out my references at the back of the book).

Roughly . . .

2 percent of the U.S. population are bipolar

70 percent of that 2 percent are depressed

.6 percent of the population are then manic

50 percent of that .6 percent have psychosis in their mania

50 percent of the .3 percent with psychosis have chronic manic episode issues

.15 percent chance I'd have this form of BMD. Well, add in the fact that I also have zero family history of bipolar disorder and that number probably shrinks even more, but I had no luck finding that obscure bipolar stat on the World Wide Web.

After I initially tracked down and put together these statistics, the feeling I had was a little tough to accurately describe. Let me try to compare it to something. OK, like let's say I'm driving down the road in my Jeep (Jeep wave) on a sunny, clear summer day when suddenly a lightning bolt strikes fifty feet in front of me with no visible signs of clouds anywhere around. The only thing going through my mind at that point (as with the statistics) is: "What the *fuck* is going on?"

I mean, how in the hell does this BMD not affect me and change me? I feel as though everything in this world is always changing. This of course would include me, and to think that I have BMD and believe I could stop this change is absolutely crazy. I have difficulty looking at the numbers above and believing that they mean nothing, that I should continue with my life and not try to change. I'm better than that now, and that's exactly how I know BMD has changed me: I no longer run from it but rather embrace it and look to it to define me.

SESSION

JP: Well, didn't they just break the mold with you.

DT: Weird. My sis is the only other person I've ever heard phrase it like that.

JP: I know; I spoke with her last night about ya.

DT: Of course you did.

ORANGE

(ELEVATED MODERATE MOODS,
SIGNIFICANT IMPAIRMENT,
ABLE TO WORK)

KEY TERMS: BLOG, CRAZY PERSON, "GOURNAL," UNDENIABLY BAD
Submitted on 6/10/09
Orange

I thought about starting this blog off with an excerpt from my "gournal." Let's just get this out there. If you:

A.) don't get the "gournal" joke/reference or

B.) refuse to think it's funny after you research it online, just stop reading right now. This will more than likely be a complete waste of your time, and this blog is better than that negativity and non-committal mentality you have.

Great, now that we've weeded out the casual readers, I'll go ahead and tell you that the above "gournal" reference is from *Wet Hot American Summer.* If you have not had the luxury of opening your mind to limitless humor for about an hour and half, I suggest you watch this movie. If you have, I challenge you to watch it with the farts option right now and come back to finish reading this. And if you have done both, well, congrats because you're officially T.A.N. I guess I should get to the point before I lose any more of you to credible blogs or websites that actually have a point, and get to it before the second paragraph: I'm bipolar and this is my medicine. There, got it in before the second paragraph. Take that, haters.

Now, let's get down to the nitty-gritty. Yes I had to google that term to make sure I used it correctly and guess what, I did. OK, sort of. I used knitty first and got a bunch of hits for baby cats, also known as kittens; man, do people go mental over kittens. In any case, I was diagnosed with manic-depressive disorder about eighteen months ago, and since then my life has been quite interesting to say the least. When I talk about being bipolar or manic-depressive (or BMD for the trendy abbreviations-minded peeps out there) people usually think I'm morbidly depressed or some kind of a crazy person. In all honesty, I would say maybe I'm a little crazy, but come to think of it, who wants to be normal? If you find a normal person who's fun to hang out with, go ahead and give up because your life is no longer interesting (that's a joke; please don't really give up but do think about making some serious changes). I wanted to start this blog to get some stuff off my chest and to hopefully laugh at how my bipolar life ends up.

As few of you know and probably fewer care about, BMD is characterized by emotional highs and lows throughout life in seemingly just about the most ridiculous occurrences and times in my life. Try to imagine the best/scariest/most thrilling roller coaster you've ever been on and multiply that by about ten. For those of you who have never been on a roller coaster, you're probably lame and aren't reading this so we should be good with that metaphor.

> Side note: For those of you who have already probably begun picking out and degrading this blog because of my poor grammar and punctuation, well, to you I say, deal with it. See, funny story about that is, my freshman year English prof actually wrote on my inspirational essay about my dad that I had dishonored my father with my poor grammar and punctuation. I've since made peace with it and moved on. So should you.

Anyway, back to my comparison. Imagine that you are in the front car of this roller coaster and slowly moving your way up the first hill when all of a sudden, right before the apex on the hill, the loudspeaker comes on and the operator of the coaster announces:

"We are sorry to inform the riders that the brakes on this ride have malfunctioned and there is unfortunately no way for us to control the roller coaster. Good luck, and we'll be pulling for you." Yeah, this could be unbelievably awesome or undeniably bad.

I've had some unbelievably awesome experiences while manic and some undeniably bad times as well. I've tried to take the medical approach of seeing psychiatrists and psychologists (yes, kids, that's right, these professions are not one and the same, I had no idea either) who have had me on a few types of meds that really didn't work for me. I've tried groups and individual therapy, but they just didn't do it for me, so I've decided that I'll try this. I mean, what's the worst that can happen? I start climbing houses and running around half-naked, trying to elude capture from the KGB? Wait, that's already happened; we'll get to those stories soon enough. So please make sure your seat belt is tight around your waist, and please keep your arms and legs inside the car during the ride (unless you wanna have a lot of fun, of course).

SESSION

JP: Roller coasters seem to be a common metaphor for bipolar disorder. It's obviously a reflection of the way bipolar disorder can take people to the highest of highs and down to the lowest of lows, rapidly and unpredictably.

DT: Yeah, it can be exhilarating and terrifying all at the same time, making you chase the manic high to the point where you uncontrollably come crashing back down to reality, so hard that it rocks you from within.

JP: Yeah, that wouldn't really agree with me. Roller coasters and I never really got along so much; that's the main reason I stopped going to Kings Island. Well, that and they took out my favorite Smurf ride.

DT: Dude, I *loved* that ride too.

KEY TERMS: NORMAL, DEPAKENE, ROLLER COASTER, BRITNEY SPEARS
Submitted on 6/11/09
Orange

I guess if you have made it this far (and by far I mean the second entry, so don't be too proud of yourself but thanks for being a loyal friend and follower) I at least owe you some idea of how I plan to lay out this blog. I first had the idea to look around the

Internet for other blogs about BMD to see how they were formatted and structured, but then realized that was a totally lame idea. I didn't want to be influenced somehow or subconsciously persuaded to follow the format of someone else's blog and steal their creative mojo. Plus, taking the time to read all those blogs just wasn't in the cards . . . OK, you got me. The time thing was the real reason, but I wanted to try and sound intelligent for a minute. My mistake. It won't happen again.

So I'm basically winging it out here and just seeing how it goes, but in my opinion I think I'm rocking it out already. After a long deliberation (otherwise known as watching *The Fresh Prince of Bel-Air* reruns and eating pizza) I've decided to write about my latest manic experience, and if there hasn't been one in a while, I'll dabble back to my gournal and let you into my first full-blown manic episode that happened last year. Try to contain your excitement; I know my hands are already shaking.

As I mentioned, I experienced my first manic episode back in 2008 while living in the quaint little mountain metropolis known as Denver, Colorado. While I won't get into the details just yet, I will say that I was provided a nice retreat for about a week, where I could get to relax and hang out with some real interesting people. Thanks, Porter Hospital Psychiatric Ward. It was during this time that I was first put on some medication to try and get me back to normal, whatever normal is.

I tried to stay on Depakene and Abilify for about eight months, but let me tell you, it was like I was one of those zombies from Michael Jackson's "Thriller" video minus the sweet dance moves. With some support, and by some I mean basically none, I decided to wean (funny word, go ahead, say it aloud . . . told you it's funny) myself off the meds and see how I did without them.

Now, if someone suffering from BMD or any other mental condition comes across this entry and decides to follow my lead, please note this disclaimer:

I am not a physician and do not have the qualifications to advise or promote anyone   to drop off their meds that were prescribed to them.

I tried an "Ask a Lawyer" website to see if I needed that disclaimer, but they needed my email and some form of payment, so I decided to pass and write that little entry down; I should be good I think (50-50). In any case, since being clean I've reverted back to the self that I know, which is good for me and even better for humanity. But as I said, I still have some experiences of mania. The first one that I'll tell you about convinced me to start this blog. Buckle up because here we go on that roller coaster.

One of the cooler aspects of my mania is that colors play a big role in what's going on. For instance, I was driving from The Nasty over to my gym to get my swell on (that's a lie; I was actually working out to try and get back into shape after gaining twenty pounds from the meds, another side effect that sucks) when I started to drift into mania. I started thinking about why this particular blue car (have no idea of make or model, but stay with me as it doesn't matter, or at least to me it doesn't) was stopped at the light in the Y crossing just in front of me.

Why was that car blue? Not the chemical reason, because I'm pretty sure that explanation is way above my head. OK, not pretty sure--I'm positive it is because I'm not sure it's even chemistry; it might have something to do with light. And why was it at that stop light at this exact time, and why was I so focused on it? The easy answers are that the driver was on their way home, and that I should get over this thing with the car. But at times I think, there's the problem, I just let things go without appreciating or thinking about what's really going on. In any case, for some reason my mind started racing about how the car was there as part of a plan that had me driving by this place at this exact time to see this blue car and trigger this ridiculous rhetoric I am now writing.

I proceeded to the gym and flew through my workout, my mind running wild with what I wanted to do in terms of starting this blog and what I wanted to write about. Bottom line: I wanted to share this craziness with the world. I convinced myself that this was not only a good idea, but probably the best idea I've had since I was manic and decided to send a dozen sunflowers to Britney Spears last year on *my* birthday (still a little disappointed that I never got a thank-you from Brit, though).

By this point, I'd decided that I should start writing about my mania experiences and had the idea of how to do it, but for some reason I was walking out of the gym, wanting some sign to tell me that I should do it. Well, let's just say that answer was quickly given to me, because the entire ride home I only saw the color blue, and I mean saw it everywhere. It started with a girl sitting in the car next to me, rockin' aviators, and blue glass paint with *my* name in her back window; and then a blue bus over there, a blue sign here, and everyone around only wearing shades of blue. Then all of a sudden I saw two police officers (that's right, believe it or not, they *are* wearing blue) cruising around on their Segways. OK, how many cops have you seen on Segways? Other than the ones at the mall, who are security guards and not cops, I mean I've seen like none. I started getting pumped up and excited, laughing and dancing all the way back to my apartment, knowing that I'd just seen my "sign." I sat down and started writing.

SESSION

JP: So by chance, can you remember any other color themes in your mania?

DT: Well, I was the color green in my mania, and I think it symbolized a new beginning or something crazy like that. My friends and emotions would also be represented by colors, and I recall my mania or evil being symbolized by the color black. I would constantly change what I was wearing to try and disguise which emotion I was actually feeling at the time. Wow, thanks for opening up that can of worms for me there, JP.

JP: You're welcome.

DT: I was being sarcastic.

JP: I don't care.

KEY TERMS: CYCLING, "INFORMER," TRIGGERS, ROCKY ROAD
Submitted on 6/16/09
Orange

In the past week or so, I've managed to somehow lose my debit card, job, parking garage entry card, and my mind. OK, OK, that may be a bit of an exaggeration, but starting out this entry with that line was irresistible; I mean, it has everything to get you hooked in.

There are the subtle, normal everyday occurrences of misplacing your debit card (or leaving it in the ATM machine Saturday night around midnight because I just *had* to beat the crowd to the bar) as well as the misplacing of the parking garage entry card. I was able to accomplish the latter in a mere six hours, a new record for myself considering it never leaves my vehicle. Then add in the dramatics of losing both my mind and job. I need to explain that I didn't really lose my job but rather made the decision to resign. I should also clarify that I didn't really lose my mind, but had probably the closest thing to another episode since Denver. You must admit, though, that these aren't nearly as climactic as my opening statement was.

I did have a couple of days last week when I was cycling so severely that I actually was a little scared. And I'm not talking about the spin classes at your local Y on Monday nights cycling either, though I can appreciate the fear involved in that as well. I'm referring to going from manic back to normal back to manic to some sort of weird low emotion back to manic to normal, over a course of a couple of days. To try and explain better: I would go from dancing my butt off in the middle of the living room, jamming to Snow's "Informer" (yes, I know, simply classic track) to crying my eyes out in the bathroom to running around The Nasty paranoid that I was being watched. Ya know, a typical case of the Mondays.

I was told that there could be triggers throughout my life that could send me into a manic state, or worse, another episode. Well, I guess I found one. This actually came in the form of my job; I had tried to go back to doing a similar job in a smaller telecom company. The funny thing (well, at least I have to laugh at it because I'm not sure how else to handle it) is there's no guidebook or directions on how to live with BMD (that I've found that are worth a damn).

While there seem to be similarities (or at least I've found similarities from a little research) with what others experience during mania, no one taken the time to actually study this and would rather try to "fix" the problem by drugging you beyond comprehension (hmmm, I'll pass). So really the only way to figure out if something is going to work is to do it, wait, and see what happens. Trying to go back to a similar work environment and a similar job just wasn't in the cards, and my mind let me know that.

The good news is that as soon as I separated myself from the triggering factors I was experiencing at work, my mania came back into check. I regained control (as much as I can have, I guess) and feel really good again. It was difficult for me to quit my job as I was doing so well, and I struggle with saying or demonstrating that I'm not able to do something. As difficult as that is, there's no doubt I would have ended up back in the hospital if I hadn't taken the necessary steps to separate myself from those triggers at work. I guess I'm just learning to deal with all of this. It's a rocky road, but at least there is a road.

SESSION

JP: Bipolar triggers are behaviors and outside events that lead to bipolar disorder symptoms. These triggers can be positive or negative. Some common triggers are alcohol and drug abuse, stressful work, travel, relationship problems, social isolation, and medication side effects. It's a good idea to track your own triggers to effectively manage them.

DT: I think the stressful work environment is one of my major triggers, but that's just one of many that I'm still working on.

JP: Taking on accountability and initiative in this will undoubtedly pay dividends throughout your treatment, getting you closer to living as happy and healthy a life as possible despite bipolar disorder. This is a great achievement, Derek, and one you should be very proud of.

KEY TERMS: CHILLS, JOHNNY DEPP, FARMHOUSE, COPPERS
Submitted on 6/25/09
Orange

How much do you like the feeling you get when you're in the middle of a dream and you're falling, falling, falling just waiting to hit the ground, when all of a sudden you wake up and those chills run up and down your spine? I for one love that feeling. It's like I'm seeing my death about to happen right in front of my eyes, and then I find myself completely safe and sound, lying in my own bed. I usually lie in bed and try to collect my thoughts after those chills, and at that point I would say I feel as alive as in any other moment.

I read somewhere (in a book) that if for some reason you don't wake up from the dream during that fall and hit the ground, you die; that if you die in any way in any of your dreams, you actually cease to live. Now, how they would be able to know that, seeing how if you die in your sleep, you can't tell someone what you were dreaming about? I'll leave that for you to ponder. If that little factoid was true, I'd say that I'd have died at least four times since last March.

My most recent dream like this happened a couple of nights ago. I'll flip it on your ass here a little bit and drop some fore-shadowing: I should be dead twice over. Since I can recall, I've always had vivid dreams that I can usually remember in detail. However, I was never killed in my dreams until after my epi-sode, and since then I've been shot, stabbed, beaten, and sliced to death. This last dream had started with me riding around with Johnny Depp, when all of a sudden he pulled a gun on me. It seems that we had just been set up, and that we were also some kind of gangsters (probably because I just saw the trailer for *Public Enemies*) in the 1930s, and now we were racing back to our hideout/home/my childhood farmhouse (makes perfect sense, doesn't it?). I did somehow convince Johnny that it wasn't me who set him up, and now we were speeding around South Chuck trying to escape from the coppers.

The next thing I can remember, we were driving on a farm and looking for a bridge to cross the creek to get over to my farmhouse. We slowed down, and all of a sudden a cop jammed his shotgun through the back window. When I turned to look, *boom*--shot right in the chest. Now, I'm no doctor, but I would imagine taking a shotgun blast in the chest from a foot away would be life-threatening, so if the aforementioned dream-death theory is true, I shouldn't be alive.

This is when it gets really weird (like it's not already). My dream paused for an instant, as if my life paused, so I thought I was dead. This lasted about a few seconds (or what I can try to guess are seconds) when suddenly I was on my knees, being yelled at to lift my arms by the coppers, but due to the buckshot in my chest I was unable to do so. Johnny Depp and the driver of our car were yelling at me to not give up any information and explaining that we were just in a wreck and that was the reason for my injuries. I ignored Johnny (mistake) and told the cops it was him; for what, I don't know, but it seemed like the right thing to do at the time. So now I had Johnny Depp wanting to kill me. Scary stuff.

Anyhow, like in any good gangster flick, we somehow escaped from the cops and ran down the creek bed, looking for a place to cross. I asked Johnny why the cops were trying to kill me, and his response was:

"For the same reason I am."

I instantly became fearful for my life again and jumped into the creek. Johnny followed, and the next thing I knew, I was being drowned by Johnny Depp in the creek that runs beside my old childhood farmhouse.

I woke up.

I have to shake my head and laugh at this ridiculous dream and try to explain that being killed in your dreams doesn't mean you die in real life (I think, but everyone pinch themselves to make sure).

SESSION

JP: There has been research about dreams and their relationships with people suffering from bipolar disorder. A particularly interesting piece of data is from a study by Beauchman and Hays: they found that bipolar patients report bizarre dreams with death and injury themes before their shift to mania. Let's see, this entry was at the end of June'09, and when did your second episode occur?

DT: November/December of that same year. That's definitely what was going on because those types of dreams occurred throughout the year. It's so crazy that there are so many commonalities and similarities uncovered in studies of people with bipolar disorder, but still no real clue about what it is.

JP: It's a complex disorder, but with the increasing efforts, research, and medical studies, I'm sure breakthroughs will occur.

DT: Now I think you're the one who's dreaming, JP. I don't think you can uncover what's not meant to be found.

JP: Why, aren't we the insightful philosopher today?

DT: Thanks. I've been working on that one for a while now, hoping to get it in the book at some point.

KEY TERMS: SKIRTS, GLIMPSES, THEY, POST-IT NOTE
Submitted on 10/08/09
Orange

First and foremost, I would like to take some time and thank the residents of Athens, Georgia for welcoming JD and me over the past weekend. It's not the easiest thing to make a Yank feel welcome in the South, and I truly appreciate the effort. I mean, asking that all the ladies wear dresses for the UGA game in our honor was more than any one man can ask for. I even saw a few wearing cowboy boots and skirts. Thank you so much.

Now, back to my original train of thought, or as close to it as possible, as I am now having issues with focusing on anything but the Southern belles from the weekend. While driving back from the ATL this weekend, I experienced glimpses back into my past at times (not weird at all). Not necessarily visions or anything cool like that, but a sign, song, car, conversation or billboard would make me recall things, like placing Post-it note reminders in my mind. At times, these occurrences would bring back to light a feeling or idea I had during my episode. For most of the time I was manic in Denver, my memory is gone; not sure if that's for my own good, but I think I'm thankful for it. The common themes and overall objective during my episode are there, but my day-to-day or hour-to-hour activities are lost. However, from time to time, like on this drive, something will pop into my head that I can relate to instantaneously.

Sometimes when this happens, it can get a little confusing and scary. Say for a split second, I'm convinced *they* are following me and I'm failing. And then at times it can be pretty fun. If you've ever had that feeling right after a crash seems imminent but somehow you miss it, you can relate. The chills and tingles are running up and down your spine and your scalp, and you feel like you cheated death. That feeling is pretty cool; at least for a crazy person like me, it is. These feelings usually pass after a few seconds, and then I'm good with my day, but then there are the bathroom times.

Bathroom times are when things might get a little much and I need to settle myself down. I don't really understand BMD or how it works, but I do know what works for me. Sure, hanging out in a bathroom doesn't sound like the most normal thing to do, but it works. For some reason, I can calm myself down in there, and I feel safer. Can't wait till my next girlfriend finds me sitting in the dark in the bathroom by myself. That'll be a fun conversation.

The reason I was investigating the décor in the bathroom in Hamilton by myself during the wedding a few weekends ago was something that was my own fault. I've come to terms with what happened during my episode, or about as close as you can, I imagine; and while it's never completely out of my mind, I'm not dwelling on it. But most of what I'm handling is what I can remember about what happened. Jazz was there among a few others during this roller-coaster ride of my episode, so I wanted to talk to him about what he saw and such. Sure, what he said freaked me out a little, about what I was doing and saying and the way I was acting. All of which I couldn't remember. To think I was that out of control is concerning. I know it all kind of caught up with me two Saturday nights ago. A date with a bathroom was bound to happen.

Sure, I could go on with my life and act like the episode never happened, and I could try to hide from BMD, but it's not going anywhere. It's a part of me now, and it really is who I am. I know there are going to be more conversations with my friends about what happened, and some are going to be harder to take than others (fact), but I need to know. I feel like I owe it to myself, because no one else is going to do it. I'm truly thankful my friends are there to help, so I'm sorry if I end up freaking you all out by shutting myself in a bathroom from time to time.

SESSION

JP: You definitely should incorporate all the discussions with your friends to describe your manic episodes in multiple points of view in your next book. It would be great.

DT: Next book? Can we focus on trying to get this one out first, big guy?

JP: I'm just saying.

KEY TERMS: KNEE FOOTBALL, TRADITION, FUNYONS, SNUGGIE
Submitted on 12/7/09
Orange

"Hello, sports fans, and welcome to 'Primetime Knee Football.' I'm Brent Musburger, and we are coming to you live today from the cornfields of central Ohio, where the locals have deemed the playing field as 'Back the Lane.' It's not unknown around these parts that the fierce competition that usually results from these epic battles between brothers runs over into the Monday morning bus stop for the Thompson Boys, but this is what keeps us coming back for more. For those of you new to the game, I'll pass it along to our resident professional, Stubby, to give you the lowdown of the game."

"Thanks, Brent. The boys usually play this game somewhere in the toy room by the 'Pop and Shot' there to the left, with the end zones being the toy tractor line to the north and the living room to the south. No pads are allowed in this game, so the boys will be on their knees for the duration, but heavy hitting and multiple name-calling are encouraged. The game usually lasts anywhere between a half-hour to an hour, depending on which brother gets upset and decides to quit. The action is always two on one, with the offense having the advantage with the extra player. Needless to say, we're in for a treat today, as some heated exchanges have already begun during pre-game when the boys were eating their breakfast and watching cartoons."

In honor of the Thompson Boys' childhood tradition of knee football, I've decided to start a new tradition with my brothers that they have no idea about, but one that I think will be a family favorite when it's all said and done. Every Christmas, we are no different from any other family--well, one that has Christmas breakfast with their mom and stepdad along with their dad at their mom's house before opening presents together. We put the funk in dysfunctional. But the manner in which we exchange gifts is ordinary. I usually try to get something for my brothers that I think they will enjoy and is popular at the time. For instance, a couple of years back, I got them iPods; nothing extravagant, but nice. I've realized that this tradition is missing something, so I've decided to make a change for the better (I hope).

Rather than exchanging traditional gifts, I've made up my mind that this year I'm going to do something a little different. I've known my brothers their entire lives and thus feel that I know them fairly well. For this reason, I've decided that every year, I'm going to give them their favorite childhood breakfast from "Primetime Knee Football" (Yoo-hoo and Honey Buns, root beer and Funyuns, I'll let you guess who gets what) along with a gift from the As Seen on TV category. Lately, I've been paying close attention to commercials to find the perfect TV gift for my brothers and found it, a Snuggie.

I know many of you are thinking that a Snuggie is a great idea, and I couldn't agree more (aside from the new dog Snuggie; a dog has fur to keep it warm, I feel it's like putting a rain coat on a duck). The reason I chose a Snuggie may not be that common, though. During my episode, I became obsessed with noticing little things throughout my surroundings. I believed that a hand gesture, the color of a bum's shirt, the background set in a movie, or the way a person greeted me were all signs or symbols leading me on a journey. Now, from time to time this feeling will creep back into me, and this happened during the Snuggie commercial.

I never noticed this before, but when the commercial cuts to the fans at a sports game all wearing Snuggies outside, there is an old man sitting in the front left-hand side towards the middle with no Snuggie on, freezing his butt off and shaking. Just rewind the commercial next time and stop it at this spot; pretty entertaining. This guy makes the whole commercial for me. It's a little sad yet downright hilarious that no one in the crowd (especially considering the fact they are all at least twenty years younger) has the decency to offer this obvious grandpa a Snuggie to ease his extreme discomfort.

A little bit of a lame reason to decide on the Snuggie, I know, but I'm glad my mania has led me to notice the little things in life more. I couldn't tell you how many toys my brothers and I received while growing up, but one of the most fun we had was playing knee football with a pillow. It's like the old man in the commercial. It's not the big flashy in-your- face elements of the commercial everyone else notices that hooked me. It was the simple, low-key, yet perfect shivering old man. As frustrated as I get with my mania, I'm glad it's around to remind me of what is important in life: a breakfast of champions with root beer, Funyuns, Yoo-hoo, and Honey Buns.

SESSION

JP: Did your brothers enjoy their sugar for breakfast this year?

DT: Yeah, I kind of decided against that tradition, considering when I bought those gifts, I was convinced I was the Wizard of Oz. I thought it best to steer clear of anything that might trigger mania again.

JP: Recognizing those triggers and avoiding them will go a long way toward living as healthy life as possible.

DT: Yeah, but I was a pretty badass Wizard of Oz though.

JP: I'm sure you were, pumpkin-head--

DT: You *really* need to stop talking with my mom about me.

KEY TERMS: LORD'S PRAYER, HALLUCINATE, APOCALYPTIC, ACE
Submitted on 1/21/10
Orange

WARNING! WARNING! WARNING! WARNING! WARNING!

I am going to use this entry to discuss religion and spirituality, so if you are easily offended by such conversation, please stop reading now.

It has been nearly a month since my last episode, and the only physical aftermath (well, aside from the scar from the cigarette burn on my palm, I should get a palm reading and see what they say about that) is the cracked dry skin between my fingers on both hands. This was caused by my obsessive need to pray during my episode. I'd guesstimate I recited the Lord's Prayer several hundred times. There are a few underlying themes that come to light during my episodes, and the dominant one (well, co-dominant, but I'm not ready to share the other quite yet) is religion/spirituality.

I (like 50 percent of all BMD manics; and yes, I asked El Doc yesterday for that stat) have been blessed with psychosis during my episodes. This means I hallucinate, am delusional, and have intense feelings of grandiosity. It's like going to bed sober and then waking up feeling like I'm on psychedelic drugs; yeah, it can get a little trippy. It fascinates me that these symptoms are so common among BMD manics. No matter where in the world one may be, the religious/spiritual symptoms are strongly similar. I've gone over this in my head countless times in the past two years, trying to find some sort of answer or clue. The same can be said for countless research studies around the globe, one of which I'm rockin' with UC right meow. For me, I believe it can be boiled down to one simple phrase: my God has one hell of a sense of humor. Right about here is where the people who didn't take my earlier warning seriously are more than likely seriously pissed.

I have to laugh at my situation because it can be just so ridiculous at times. My mania can feel like a game inside my head where all the rules of the natural world are thrown out the window and it feels like my life is at stake, plus the lives of all of humanity. Apocalyptic feelings aren't real fun. I have to laugh at it in hindsight due to how ridiculous it sounds. I heart using analogies/metaphors (I always use them interchangeably and incorrectly so figured I'd just drop them both in there) so here's one: it can feel like I'm sitting down to play a single hand of poker with the Devil and my soul is at stake. The dealer deals out the cards and somehow I'm playing with UNO cards and the re-deal rule doesn't exist. Lucky for me, I've got an ace up my sleeve.

One of my questions during my research interviews at UC (ooooooohhhh, ooooooohhhh, ooooooohhhh, clap, clap, clap, U-C!) centers around if I believe I have a special relationship with God that others cannot have. The first few times I heard this question (I had to answer it every time for ten sessions) I responded by saying no. I didn't want to think that I was somehow better than anyone else by implying that my relationship with God was some kind of exclusive arrangement. But after thinking about it the past couple of weeks, I do think I have a special relationship with God that no one else can have, and I also think everyone else should think that way. I can't begin to try and imagine what the other billions of people in the world are going through. I mean, right now the entire country of Haiti is suffering beyond belief. I believe that God works with them in a way that they need and only they can understand. If our relationships with God weren't special and were all the same, then we'd all have nothing.

I can't stop smiling and laughing at some of the things I've experienced in the past couple years of my life that at first glance seem absolutely absurd. For instance, during episode deuce, my belief that I had put the phone company on hold and was playing a global game of hide-and-seek, all while pulling a practical joke on the entire planet. But in the end, I'm going to get the last laugh. Because I'm counting on making my hand of UNO cards to dominate that poker game with old Lucifer, even if I do have to cheat and get a lot of help from my Ace upstairs.

SESSION

JP: You have this ranked as an elevated mood with moderate severity; I'm interested in why you put it there?

DT: Well, I can remember how it felt for the first month or so after getting out of the hospital. I wasn't having any psychotic symptoms, hallucinations or anything, but my dreams were unlike anything I'd ever had before. I would even dream that I was manic.

JP: Have you always had bad dreams?

DT: Not really. After my first episode, they started coming more often.

JP: What type of nightmares?

DT: Well, like, I'd watch my brothers or some other close family members die in front of me. I've been killed in my dreams as well.

JP: How do you deal with these?

DT: I write about them. It's my way of fighting back.

KEY TERMS: CHANDLER, RECEPTIONIST, TEACHER'S PET, STANFORD
Submitted on 6/7/10
Orange

I have been fortunate enough to receive a new nickname to add to my list: Chandler. Yes, a couple of my new coworkers (well, I'm an intern but give me a break, you're about to see why) have decided that since I'm old (twenty-nine, not that old) and an intern that my nickname is Chandler from *Friends* (except I don't get to sleep with that smokin' Cougar). I of course laughed at the nickname and honestly didn't mind it, and was having some fun that day with everything until I learned of my upcoming tasks for a couple of weeks this summer--as a receptionist.

I totally understand that I'm starting from the bottom of the totem pole once again, but this BMD will flare up, and when it comes out, it's usually just to my parents, but why should they have all the fun (I'll leave out the tears for you all, though)? Of course, I'll go along with the joke and everything, but there is a small part of me that would like to let them know what I'm thinking.

"Never mind the fact that I, a mere two years ago, was the up-and-coming talent, on my way to the top of a company of over 300K employees. Or that I've managed a $5 million annual module, which is a third of the total sales revenue this company brought in last year. I wasn't driving an X5 (Big Body Beamer) or approved for a $300K home loan. Just ignore the fact that I was overtaking the top performing module in Silicon Valley. I wasn't looking at returning to school at a little-known university on the West Coast: Stanford (maybe you've heard of it, or at least seen their tree mascot). No, no, I wanted to leave all of this entirely behind to come and answer your phones. Where's the transfer button again?"

Of course I'd never say this, but it would feel really good. Don't get me wrong; I'm very proud of myself for getting this far. I mean, in those same two years, I've been hospitalized twice (in a psych ward, that's like double jeopardy or something), fought depression off twice, was lucky enough to overcome suicidal thoughts and intentions, and have picked myself up off the ground more times than I'd like to count. But I can't tell them any of this, not necessarily because I'm afraid that I'd lose any opportunity for a potential job (this is what I always thought before) but because I don't feel I should need to tell them.

For the longest time, I cared too much about what others thought of me, before and after my episodes. Recently, I was telling my parents what a tough time I'm having. I'm not sure if it is a combination of moving to a new city, starting a new career (well, attempting to), dealing with finding healthcare (practically impossible, thanks, preexisting condition), and not giving myself time to recover. Six days after I got out of the hospital, I was back in class. Can anyone say teacher's pet?

I don't have the answer to any of this, and I'm not real sure if anyone does. But I refuse to quit. I'm not sure where I'll end up, but I have to keep grinding. If I stop caring, then eventually no one will care; that's the furthest thing from what I want.

. . . I just reread this entry and realized it makes very little sense. I'd better keep an eye on that . . .

SESSION

JP: I think the most telling part of this entry isn't the structure of it, but rather when you listed the possible reasons why you were having a tough time. It seems like your ambition, which is usually seen as a positive attribute, can hurt you by pushing when you probably need to settle down. Does this sound right?

DT: Definitely. It's something I struggle with constantly. I know I have the talent, skill, work ethic, drive and ambition to be successful in the corporate environment, so I pushed too hard to get back. I mean, I enjoyed it as well and took pride in my work and career. I saw it as a direct reflection of myself and as something I felt I could control more than anything; I felt I had no excuse for failure. Now, that seems to get me in trouble because of the BMD variable. I simply can't do what I used to be so good at.

JP: Whether you realize it or not, ambitiousness is still a good quality to have. Now you just have to learn to adjust to accommodate bipolar disorder. Finding activities that are rewarding in different ways to replace those you mentioned above can be a good start.

KEY TERMS: ARMAGEDDON, JUDAS, MANIA, CURE
Submitted on 6/10/11
Orange

As I've mentioned, there is no cure for BMD, but the lithium does seem to help. So far, so good. Seeing as how lithium is not the cure, my mania still decides to come out and play every once in a while. One of these times happened last week, when mania decided to take my mind on a little journey. While I may not have physically left the present, my mind was undoubtedly at Armageddon.

In case some of you have forgotten what you learned from church or wherever, I'll review the story of Armageddon real quick. Despite Hollywood's best efforts to redefine Armageddon, it's an actual geographic place and not a frickin' giant asteroid no one is able to see until we have like two weeks till impact (yet the Hubble Telescope is capable of looking back into time; yeah, my ass, Hollywood). It's on a hill in Israel known as Megiddo and overlooks the Jezreel Valley (I totally had to look that up) where the Antichrist gathers the world's rulers for battle. Basically the end of time, if you're a real pessimist.

Well, to sum up the introduction here, my mania sent me to this hill, and while there I was fighting the Antichrist, due to the fact that I was a soldier of the light in episode uno (that kind of thing carries over from manic experience to manic experience). JC is coming down from heaven to save the day, and my mania puts the present-day me right in the middle of this situation, and my dialogue goes something like this:

"JC! Where the hell have you been, man? We've been getting slaughtered down here, literally. Look at all the bodies, it's not good. I mean, how are you so late? It's not like you don't have the best seat in the house or anything. You're God's son and you were *up* in heaven; I'm really confused about how you missed all of this going on down here. I mean, honestly, how couldn't you know what was going on? What gives? We obviously need a ton of help here with this asshole.

"What? You overslept?!? OK, who was supposed to wake up Jesus?

"Judas? Really, man? I mean, given the past and everything, you think you'd be on top of something important like this. You really screwed us here again, didn't ya, bud?

"Wait, JC, all you brought was a sword? You're kidding, right?

"Oh, you were running behind because of Judas, so you only had time to grab a sword, huh? That's just great. Well, let's just hope the Antichrist doesn't have a shield or anything.

"CHHHHAAAAAAAAAAAAARRRRRRRRGE!!!!!"

I've read that many people who suffer from mania have some issues giving it up. That they will quit their meds in the hope of again feeling the rush from mania. I can see myself falling into this frame of mind at times. I do love my mania because it's taken me places that no one else in this world has ever been before. I have seen things that I didn't think were possible to see, and to say I could give all of that up and not want it back is crazy. I just have to learn that like most things in life, moderation is the determining factor in how good or how bad things can get with my mania. Easier said than done, I'm afraid.

SESSION

JP: How long will one of these manic experiences last, like the one you are explaining in this entry?

DT: It depends on my mood at the time, what I'm doing, how much I'm enjoying the ride, and what's going on in the experience. The Armageddon experience above only lasted about thirty seconds, but I was driving at the time, so that factor played heavily in the length of time.

JP: Driving while manic? That can't be real safe.

DT: Sometimes I'm just along for the ride, JP; holding on and simply trying to make it back.

RED
(ELEVATED SEVERE MOODS,
SIGNIFICANT IMPAIRMENT,
UNABLE TO WORK)

<u>KEY TERMS:</u> DOCUMENTARY, FLOBOTS, d0lroK, "BUGS"

Submitted on 6/18/09
Red

I can be absolutely dumbfounded from time to time, and one of those occurrences happened today when I tried to purchase a documentary from a Best Buy near The Nasty. Now, I'm not trying to point fingers or make any assumptions about the intellect of our neighbors to the South, but I was in Kentucky at this time. I will also state for the record that I did not attempt to visit any other nearby Best Buys to research this event, due to the fact that I just gave up. To be fair, I wasn't exactly looking for the meaning of life or anything as important as that. I simply wanted to find a documentary called *The Devil and Daniel Johnston* which is about a singer-songwriter and artist diagnosed with BMD. I know, look at me, actually taking a proactive approach to learning more about this crazy ride I'm on. Let me paint you a picture with my prose paintbrush.

OK, I know the last line about prose painting is corny, but at first I thought it sounded cool. In any case, let me get back to my story: So I was looking online for some BMD documentaries or whatnot and found this documentary that looked really interesting, *The Devil and Daniel Johnston*. Well, interesting compared to my other options, which incorporated Van Gogh, Patty Duke, Margot Kidder, and Stephen Fry. While at some point I'll probably try to watch them all, I was really into the Daniel Johnston one because he's a musician, and music usually plays a pretty big role in my mania.

So I'm driving to this Best Buy and I'm jamming to Flobots (could quite possibly be my new fave) and maybe getting a little manic. I wouldn't say anything too crazy, just my heart racing, blood pressure up, dancing in the car, singing (or my attempt at it) and enjoying the ride. I end up at this Kentucky Best Buy and spend the next ten minutes looking for a DVD documentary section, with no luck, mind you. I mean, I could find the final season of *Knight Rider* and *Hip Hop Abs 8*, but let's not do something crazy and include a few documentary movies there.

I'm not trying to say that if they had a documentary section of DVDs, they'd make any money from it, but I mean, I do feel that at least some people out there are interested in the world beyond flat abs and cars that talk. Then again, this is the country in which someone funded the movie *Idiocracy*, so what can you expect? OK, I'll stop going off on my tangent as it may be I'm still a little manic and going off over absolutely nothing, but I feel I have a point here; probably not a good one but a point nonetheless.

Seeing how over the past couple of days, I've been as close to "normal" as I think I can be, I thought I'd talk a little about my manic episode back in the mountains last year. I figured I'd start out with why I sign off each entry with the name d01roK, seeing how that really isn't my name, and I think it's a pretty good place to start. Please be warned that my memory of my episode encompasses only about two hours from a span of around three weeks, so the details may be a little fuzzy. I did keep my gournal, but you can imagine how that turned out. You'll understand once we start getting into what was going on during the episode (hint: all over the damn place).

Anyway, during my episode, I had some experiences in which I was convinced that I was part of some universal battle between good and evil. You may want to ask me: was it like being stuck in the movie *Spaceballs*? My reply is yes, except it was nothing like it because that would have been amazing. Mel Brooks is a genius. Don't believe me? *Blazing Saddles* and *Young Frankenstein*; 'nuff said.

So this battle going on in my mind would somehow translate in the real world in the following form:

I had chosen to be on the good side during my walk (another story) and now was some sort of soldier/guardian/protector of the light or good (stay with me; I know). During my initiation into this role, I think (I repeat, the details are a little fuzzy) I was convinced I was going through some sort of universal test to prove my worth. Part of this test was that I would feel like I was always being watched or stalked, like the evil/dark/opposition/ whatever my enemy was would be keeping "bugs" on me, trying to prove I was a fraud and didn't deserve to be called good.

In order to prove this wasn't so and I wasn't scared of them, I started a YouTube account. The screen name I came up with was d01roK--almost as if it was my new manic identity--to add favorites to my profile that would portray what I was feeling at the time. I was trying to prove that I was worth the role I had been given. Essentially, I knew what was going on, and this was my way of outsmarting and outmaneuvering the enemy. Maybe at some point I'll try to tackle the meaning behind the videos, but let's just say they're pretty random, ranging from the "Handlebars" music video to the Lipton Iced Tea commercial with Rocky Balboa. Also throw in there some Penn & Teller with the American flag burning. Really weird stuff.

After taking a closer look at the name that I used for my YouTube profile, I do have some idea of why I chose it. I was at one point nicknamed D-rok, so the root of the name kind of makes sense. The 01 also makes a little sense once I think about it. During my episode, I can recall stints when I got obsessed with mathematics and time and how they related in terms of my and everyone else's existence. I recall thinking that time is just an "invention" or "method" developed by mankind to keep track of what we call life, as if our lives were defined by time. Man, that sounds weird, but it's what was going on in my head then.

In my theoretical explanation of time and mankind's relationship, there are two genders in existence (male and female in case you were wondering). If there are two genders, then they must somehow be related to time (how I believed we measured our existence). Therefore, there would have to be numerical designations for male and female in order for the mathematical formula of life to work and for time and existence to be real; hence the 0 and 1. In my mind, there were in essence only two numbers, and the rest were results of the two. Meaning, there is either nothing, which is 0 or something, which is 1. Thereby, any other number is a combination of the two.

To try and stop a confusing explanation from giving you more of a headache, I'll just say the 01 in the name had to be some way of proclaiming that I understood how or deserved to win the fight because I had figured out the equation of life and time. Mind bottling, isn't it? Why the K is capitalized and the d isn't, I have no idea, and that's probably a good thing.

SESSION

DT: I remember now why the d is lower case and the K is capitalized. It was my attempt to use symbolism to illustrate that there is no beginning and no end; that they are the same. Just as in a circle, each and every other point is both the beginning and the end, as was my life and all points of time within it. I believed I had solved the equation of time, and to show this, the d was lower case and the K was capitalized, symbolizing that they are interchangeable just like points on a circle and the points of time in my life.

JP: How did you remember all of that all of a sudden?

DT: TF's Trailer Park Grape.

KEY TERMS: TWO ROADS DIVERGED

Submitted on 6/30/09

Red

February 15 or so, 2008 (trippy manic flashback):

"Two roads diverged --"

"Two roads diverged in a yellow---"

"I took--"

"Two roads diverged in a yellow wood and--"

Each step I took, these words raced through my mind. I was on my own pilgrimage, navigating my way through reality into my new calling.

"Two roads diverged in a yellow wood and I took the one less traveled by--"

I had been on my way downtown to meet up with a couple of friends at a bar, but that objective was now far in the back of my mind. I was sitting at home when suddenly the spin began. My father was in town, and it was he who started me down this revelation; I had to complete it. I started my walk down Twentieth Street and suddenly found myself in front of some sort of Federal building; I took out my phone and snapped pictures of both sides of the Great American Seal posted on opposite sides of the entrance.

"They're watching you, leave inconspicuously."

I turned and started to walk down the road, stumbling from side to side, thinking to myself that they had no idea what I was up to. When they ran the surveillance tape the next day, they'd just see a drunk.

"I took the one less traveled by and that has made--"

I nodded and smiled at the passing Native American decent man riding a bike. He ignored my attempt to connect and sped by. I was stunned that the one person who I believed had an undeniable link to nature and appreciation for acceptance could ignore me. Was I supposed to be doing this? I stopped and found myself directly under a tree; the branches were bare and weak from the winter. I snapped a couple of pictures with my phone as evidence and moved on.

"Sometimes you are the shepherd and sometimes you are the flock."

I was now walking with no destination in mind, just walking and listening. I didn't stop at crossroads but instead turned west or north or east or south, depending on which way the cross-walk signals sent me. I was losing control but felt at ease with it.

"Two roads diverged in a yellow wood--"

I was wearing sandals and it was the middle of winter; these were my links to the past. I was beginning my walk, my journey just as so many had before me. Sometimes you have to walk through the mess of mud and despair so that others may have a better way. At this point, I was walking off the side of the sidewalk while the downtown crowd passed me on their way to the bars.

"Wow, that guy can't even stay on the sidewalk; what a drunk."

I hadn't had a drink all day. Suddenly I spotted a man and woman fighting in a car in a parking lot on my right. I did not want to draw attention to myself, so I nonchalantly glanced from time to time in their direction. I took out my phone and pretended to talk on it, describing my location to the party on the other end of the phone; it wasn't even on. I continued this act for what seemed like forever; timelessness began to take its role. The fight stopped, and I continued on my walk. From behind me, a bumper fell off a van that was part of a recent five-car crash.

"Just when you think it's over, it's just the beginning."

I turned around and the man made eye contact. He jumped off the woman in the passenger seat, threw the car in reverse and sped out of the parking lot. Did I just pass the first test? Did I stop something horrible that was about to happen? Was this why I was sent here?

I sat down on a stoop and cried.

"Two roads diverged in a yellow wood and I took the one less traveled by and that has made all the difference."

I was somehow standing in front of a clock tower in downtown. It was only myself and my thoughts, not another soul around.

"You have a choice to make; you can either head west towards the bad, evil, corrupt, and vain, the selfish temptations. Or head east towards the good, unselfishness, light, and charity for others."

"Two roads diverged . . ."

I walked home, towards the light.

SESSION

DT: I'd say at this point, I was about as manic as I could be during episode uno and still able to remember the details. I was definitely in the spin.

JP: Is the presence of good versus evil common in your mania?

DT: Yeah, it plays a very significant role.

JP: Have you explored any "spiritual emergency" or like explanations for this?

DT: Yeah, but unfortunately I'm not a shaman, just bipolar.

KEY TERMS: WILMA, BIBLICAL VERSE, TRANQUILIZER, SANDALS RESORT
Submitted on 7/6/09

March 4 or so, 2008 to March 10 or so, 2008 (trippy manic flashback):

Her name was Wilma, and she sat alone in a corner of the room with a blanket around her frail body and a lifeless gaze in her eyes. His name was Paul, and he paced around every inch of the ward, mumbling Biblical verse after Biblical verse with a look of pure confusion on his face. These two would put a real smile on my face, one that I hadn't had for what seemed like a long, long time.

It was 8:00 a.m. and breakfast was being served, or I should say you grabbed the tray with your name on it. I was still be-fuddled at this point about how my name was there because I didn't recall ordering anything. I was suddenly sent back to ju-nior high at lunchtime, when your social standing depended on your next choice: where to sit. There were about ten tables, each with a number of people sitting and talking and enjoying their time together. Then I spotted Wilma. She sat alone at the corner table with a look of total distrust and paranoia. I wish I could say I chose to sit with Wilma because I somehow knew I was sup-posed to, or that I could see she needed help. But the truth of the matter was I didn't know one single person in the ward aside from Wilma, and there weren't many seats open, so I sat down.

Wilma and I shared the distinct honor of being admitted to the suicide watch hall of the psych ward. I had been admitted a couple days prior and spent most of the next day sleeping, thanks to tranquilizers and the average of three hours of sleep a night I had been getting for the past couple of weeks; thanks, mania.

For those of you who haven't had the opportunity to spend some time in a suicide watch room on a psych ward, it's kind of like a night at a Sandals resort, with some key differences. You don't have a view of the ocean; instead, you look out the window to see a brick building about three feet away. The king-size bed with soft fresh linens and an abundance of plush pillows is ex-changed for a single bed with one sheet, pillow minus the pillow case, and a metal frame bolted to the tiled floor. The hand carved cabinets are nowhere to be found; your clothes are thrown on the floor. The whirlpool tub is replaced with a seat-less toilet (stay classy, Porter Hospital). Oh yeah, one more thing: the intimate privacy you so desire at Sandals. Well, instead, let's go ahead and put a surveillance camera right on you all the time-- perfect for anyone who's paranoid they are being watched.

Wilma's room was a few doors down from mine, and I had passed her from time to time when I managed to awake from my drug-induced slumber to use the shower (solid connection, I know).

Wilma didn't say much at first. It was as if she was so weak and tired that she could barely muster enough energy to lift the fork to her mouth. I tried to make small talk, but to no avail. She was terrified of me, of everyone and everything. She got up and walked away, and I sat there and thought to myself that even with the total chaos in my life the past few weeks, I was still happy to be alive and wanted to continue to live. I wasn't sure Wilma could say the same thing. It was hard to imagine what life events could totally crush someone to the point that they seemed as though they had given up.

Over the next few days, Wilma and I ate together, and her defenses came down a little, probably because I shared my milk with her at every breakfast. She actually began to talk to me a bit, but nothing huge. I never found out where she was from, why she was there, what had happened to her to get her to this point of her life, and I'm not sure I really wanted to know; I'm not sure I could have handled it. But in the next days, I could slowly see the life coming back into her eyes.

One morning, I woke up and started walking down to the shower when I saw Wilma dancing around the halls. I had to do a double take because I knew this could not be the same woman who could barely feed herself a few mornings ago. One of her friends had brought her a Discman and a CD. The next day, I stood by and watched Wilma dance out the ward doors with her headphones on her ears, a smile on her face, and life back in her eyes.

I smiled and thought to myself, if she can get through this, there's no reason I can't. I finally smiled.

TBC . . .

SESSION

DT: I wonder at times whatever happened to Wilma. I like to thank she's still dancing around somewhere.

JP: Do you feel a bond or connection with those patients you met on the psych ward?

DT: Unquestionably, there's something there. When we played Pictionary during my stay in Denver, one of the other patients and I were unstoppable. I mean, he'd draw a single line, and I'd yell out it was a stop sign before the ink dried. Seriously, we dominated and nobody could touch us. So you can go and put that in your pipe and smoke it!

JP: Not really what I was referring to but still quite intriguing . . .

JP: So, you gonna get that pipe out or . . .

KEY TERMS: REVELATION, SUICIDE, ROOFSLIDE, AMAZING
Submitted on 9/17/09
Red

February ??, 2008 (trippy manic flashback):

The cool, crisp morning-chilled air brushed up against my face and tickled my toes through my flip-flops. I took a deep breath and my eyes opened to focus on the northern horizon. The sun crept over the rooftops to my right as the eastern skies opened up to a new morning in the mountains. I was at peace for a moment as the world seemed to stand still, awaiting my next move, thought and revelation. The few birds that have toughed out the winter began to chirp as the new day approached. It was late February of a leap year, and aside from that I had no need or desire to know what actual time, day, or year it was. I had been chosen, like many others, to complete a mission of utter importance for the good of all mankind, and I would not fail.

The shadows from the house rooftop on which I sat blanketed the light snow dust that had accumulated on the southern side behind me. I looked out over paradise, upon an urban kingdom that rested at the feet of the giant mountains to my left. The mountains carved a symbolic crown in the western skyline. It had become clear to me that my destiny lay within the streets of the city, just as it had lain within the rural dirt roads of those who came before me. The city came alive in front of my eyes, but I heard no sounds and felt only pure ecstasy from my revelation. My heart began to race, and my mind filled with thoughts and ideas deriving from a place I could not even try to imagine. The time was now, the time was ours, and we had to empower others towards the greater good.

I looked around at the rooftops surrounding me, expecting to see the others sitting atop the apexes together, but I was alone. I slid down the southernmost snow-covered rooftop and thrust my arm out, swung through the gap between the chimney and support beam and snapped back--

"How did I get on top of this roof, and how am I not lying on the ground or metal stairwell below right now?"

15 to 20 percent of individuals with BMD commit suicide each year. This is a rough estimate, but I think it makes my point; trust me, I'll get to it. To say I didn't battle the demons inside me with suicidal thoughts and dangerous actions would be a lie. But for some reason, I am still here today when many others who share my diagnosis are not, and from time to time I ask myself why I was spared.

It takes every bit of strength in me to not react hastily and aggressively to anyone I encounter who calls suicide selfish. Until you have walked down the seemingly endless dark abyss inside your own mind that accompanies suicidal thoughts, how can you pass judgment on anyone who has? But I'm not going to stand on my soapbox and preach to you about this as I've got a brighter side to convey, and I was merely hoping to maybe broaden someone's horizons or something smart-sounding like that.

I survived my dance with suicide, as well as my tempting of fate like the above passage during my episode in Denver. I can recall a few instances during my episode where death seemed imminent, whether by a car crash or falling from a rooftop. However, I am still here, and for a while I couldn't understand why. I struggled to understand why someone or something or whatever you want to call it decided I deserved to live, because I know I was not in control of that outcome. I haven't had the desire to speed 100 miles per hour down Broad Street in Denver at noon since my episode, or had the urge to climb an unknown snow-covered rooftop in my flip-flops and roof-slide back down. I do have the feeling that I now have a second chance at life and I want to make the most of it.

I want nothing more than to try and enjoy every day and make it amazing. I know what many of you are thinking, that every day can't be amazing, but I disagree. Before my episode, I put "amazing" up on a pedestal and thought it could only be accomplished by meeting nearly impossible goals. I assumed that amazing was reserved for the rarest of times during almost unthinkable situations. But I think I was wrong; I think an amazing day can be one of the simplest and easiest things to achieve. I think it can be achieved by simply saying hello to and smiling at a neighbor or opening the door for a stranger. It's amazing how you can make someone's day by performing the smallest acts of kindness.

SESSION

JP: There are even studies that show nearly 50 percent of people with bipolar disorder attempt suicide. If someone close to you is bipolar, please be aware of warning signs such as talking about suicide; making comments about being hopeless, helpless, or worthless; switching suddenly from being very sad to being very calm or appearing to be happy; and tying up loose ends or putting their affairs in order. You need to intervene.

DT: A good friend has to do some of the toughest things imaginable at times. Get help for your friend. They'll thank you later.

KEY TERMS: TRIPPY MANIC FLASHBACK
Submitted on 10/21/09
Red

<u>February 21 or so, 2008 (trippy manic flashback)</u>:
"What, you don't think California has good schools? Stanford is right up the road; wouldn't you want to go there?"
                    —(Radio Edit), AT&T San Jose Sales Manager

I must admit, I had never dreamed that one day I would have
the opportunity to even consider attending a school as presti-
gious as Stanford, but now it was becoming a reality. I would
never have thought that a small-town farm kid from rural Ohio
could someday have a chance to walk the same grounds as some
of the most respected people in the U.S. I had felt something
different about myself dating back to the middle of January,
when Poncho and Tater visited, but I had no idea it could evolve
into this. I was on my way to San Jose to find a place to live and
check out my new office and possibly tour what could be my
new campus at Stanford. I was blessed.

I stepped onto the train at the Denver airport to head towards Delta's terminal, and the spin hit me all at once. The colors from all of the lights brightened, and the train stop bells
chimed loudly in my ears. I was suddenly overcome with a feeling of total awareness. Time seemed to slow down and my mind
cleared, allowing for deep understanding of everything that was
happening around me. I closed my eyes, leaned my head back
and smiled, took a deep breath and let the spin take control of
me.

This was my own journey, and the excitement engulfing me
was almost too much to control. I had to maintain composure
though, or the spin would be all gone after it had barely started.
I knew that in order to balance these feelings, I must involve
everyone around me, particularly my family. For it was they who
had prepared me for this journey my entire life, and now I owed
it to them to fulfill it.

Airports were the portals between perceived reality and the
secrets hidden in plain sight around us. Knowing this, I slowed

down so I could see the true meanings behind all that surrounded me. The trick to this was to be aware but appear totally oblivious. I could feel the energy and emotions rising steadily within me as I lost control. I was being guided to places throughout the airport, as if my family were leading me on my path. It almost became too much. I almost blew my composure, but then I looked up and saw I was standing in front of my savior.

"Twenty-minute massages in the airport, relax while you wait."

It seemed like a sign, symbol or message. I had never in my life received a paid-for massage, and I smiled as I knew this must be a gift. My heart was racing. I knew I needed to settle down before I boarded the plane or I could cause a catastrophe. I waited my turn and willingly but nervously took my seat. I closed my eyes and drifted away.

As the masseuse worked her way around my neck and back, my mind traveled further and further away. I was overtaken by complete relaxation, yet my mind was moving faster than I ever thought possible. Suddenly fear came rushing into me and I jolted up from the seat.

"Now I'm going to have to start all over for you," the masseuse suggested.

I was overcome with guilt as I realized what my actions had undone: she was with me and with us, and I had postponed the next part of my journey by not finishing the massage. I apologized in a manner that conveyed my message of unity and sat back down. She completed her task, and I thanked her wholeheartedly and made my way to the gate.

TBC . . .

SESSION

JP: Researching this entry, I found that conspiracy theories about the Denver International Airport are rampant, ranging from a secret underground military base, to "one world" military order depicted in the murals, to unusual words cut into the floor being Satanic, Masonic, or just some impenetrable secret code of the New World Order. There is also a dedication marker in the airport allegedly inscribed with the Square and Compasses of the Freemasons, along with a listing of the two Grand Lodges of Freemasonry in Colorado.

DT: Freemasons, you say? No wonder I was convinced they were following me. Sneaky bastards.

KEY TERMS: NEW YEAR'S EVE, "FIGHTING," PRICKS, HELP
Submitted on 1/3/10
Red

New Year's has never been one of my favorite holidays (I always fancied, yeah I said fancied, big whoop, St. Patty's Day) but this past New Year's Eve is one that I will soon not forget. As I've mentioned, I've prided myself on "fighting" BMD with no help from meds. For reasons that are beyond my comprehension-- OK, that's BS, you called me on it. For reasons that I was afraid to admit to myself, I refused help.

Call it my manly instinct (a.k.a. how to pick up chicks instinct). I was under the belief that I could conquer BMD all by myself. I was convinced that if I could live my life without meds, I would be making some profound statement about just how manly I was. The idea of my hypermasculinity is easily refuted by an examination of my immense fear of pricks; needles, that is. I was under the assumption that I was somehow stronger than I really was. The past few days have opened my eyes, once again.

I am writing this entry from the hospital, for my mania has gotten the best of me. The past few days, I have experienced things that words cannot adequately describe. I had another episode and am fighting to understand it.

Since episode uno, I have tried to beat BMD by writing, working out (the scenery isn't bad at the gym) and trying to be happy, but that just isn't enough. I've read blogs by others stating how they've overcome BMD med-free, and I envied and imitated them; I even posted a video in support of this path. However, I am only human (I think . . .). I can admit when I'm wrong and ask for help. I need *all* the help I can get.

They say New Year's is a time of new beginnings, resolutions, change. Maybe that's why I disliked New Year's so much. I didn't want to admit I was weak and needed to change. Funny how my mind can play tricks on me; if I had to guess, I'd bet my mind loves Halloween. Lately, I have said some things and acted in ways that I never thought were in me. Am I proud of these things? To a degree, I am, which leads to even more questions, but it makes me smile because I would hate to get to that point in my life when I thought I no longer needed answers.

There is a single question on my mind right meow though, and I hope the answer to it comes soon. Will my new medicine help me? Deep down, I hope and believe it will but only time will tell, and I am now grateful that I still have that time to wait and see. Happy New Year (this holiday is slowly climbing up my chart, BTW).

SESSION

JP: I'm not a big fan of New Year's, either. I can't even remember the last kiss I got at midnight; I'd have to say it was at least a couple of years ago.

DT: Shit, that's nothing. Mine was like ten years ago. And I immediately regret admitting that.

JP: Yeah, you probably should.

KEY TERMS: REFS, EUPHORIC, ENLIGHTENMENT, PUZZLES
Submitted on 1/12/10
Red

December 27, 2009 (trippy manic flashback):

The TV was on but I had little to no interest in what was showing. I was more concerned with the game being played between my reality and the perceived truths of the "outside" world. I had tried to watch the game earlier that day, but every time I concentrated on it, I adversely affected the outcome. Players were dropping like flies and the controllers of the game, the refs, had been compromised and this totally disgusted me. It was a cruel and devious act to take away one of my ultimate pleasures, and one for which I would seek revenge.

The tingling now began to slowly travel up my spine and down my legs, and I smiled as the feeling was beyond euphoric. I looked to the clock and the "time" read a quarter till midnight, the same time I stopped at the clock tower in Denver. I took a deep breath as it had suddenly become clear: this was the second and final phase of my enlightenment journey. I was but a single pawn in the game of life, being torn apart from the inside out in the name of good versus evil. An orgasmic energy to the tenth power overcame me, and I was in a state of complete ecstasy. I took out a cigarette, slid open the glass door, lit it and inhaled, trying to bring back the calm. I exhaled, turning west to east, and as the smoke mixed with the moisture from my mouth, it formed a symbolic hazy mist around the lifeless and leafless tree directly in front of me. I took a number of hits as I began to center myself again, as the realization that this was all just the beginning of the end overtook me. I glanced at the clock and it was midnight. I took the half-smoked cigarette, opened my right hand, and put the cigarette out in the middle of my palm. The nail was now gone and the revelation was now complete. I grabbed the ice-cold railing outside the door with both hands and squeezed. The pain and relief overtook me while life reentered me . . .

Present Day:
6
144
8,640
518, 400

Those are the number of days, hours, minutes and seconds I had the distinct pleasure of spending in the hospital after my last episode. Please do not feel bad for me as I do not feel bad for myself. Bizarre as it may sound, there is some fun involved when you're convinced you're the Wizard of Oz and the world is your battleground, but that's a bedtime story I'm saving for that special someone. I am writing this not to try and prove a point or to make a huge statement of some sort, but because I feel it's the right thing to do.

Now, to actually believe it's the right thing to do is a whole other story, especially when you take into consideration the above trippy manic flashback. When I was manic, the things I did seemed like the right things to do. I can get a little confused sometimes, although I can usually have fun trying to figure something out in my confusion; for example, trying to date a Southern belle. Once again, I am babbling without getting to the point, so I'll jump to the conclusion.

On my final day at the hospital, I was speaking with the doctor in charge of my unit (Southside!) and he said a key to handling BMD is to have a plan. This for me is good and bad. Unfortunately, I have an issue with overplanning everything, but we'll get to that at some other point. I did have a plan for the doctor that encompassed canceling my Denver trip (totally sucked for multiple reasons, but most notably because I had tickets to the Cavs vs. Nugs game and it was a great game), picking up old hobbies I had forgotten about (puzzles rock), heading back to school, and writing.

The doc felt all my ideas were good and even complimented me on my positive and accepting demeanor with BMD (thank you very little). However, he advised me not to post my writing on the Web. His intentions and insights were good but I feel narrow in scope, or at least that's the story that makes me feel better. His belief was that it could only be detrimental to me, due to the negative stereotypes and stigmas associated with BMD (as well as other mental health issues).

I can sympathize with the doc's view but only up to a point. I do understand that there is a chance an employer may someday find this blog and terminate me, or it could prevent me from getting a job in the first place. I'm not a complete fool, I just play one in my manic episodes. The issue conveyed to me is that we as a society do not know much about BMD; therefore, we do not talk about it and instead attach detrimental labels to people who suffer from the disorder. So in theory, by keeping this private, I would be benefiting myself.

Right there is the problem. If no one talks about it, then how is anything ever going to change? It simply can't, and I refuse to be ashamed of something that I did nothing to deserve. Will this blog and my mania prevent me from achieving my dreams? No way. It may mean I take a different path to get there, but I'm going to enjoy the ride. Who knows what can happen?

SESSION

JP: The trippy manic flashback is obviously expressing delusional thoughts, a primary symptom of a severe elevated mood, and you are quite obviously in a manic episode. You referenced time with quotation marks. Was there any significance to this?

DT: Yeah, time becomes a fairly significant theme in my manic episodes. It defies logic and reason, with hours feeling like minutes and seconds feeling like days. I can get lost in chasing it, which results in the feeling of "time" or timelessness setting in.

KEY TERMS: TRIPPY MANIC FLASHBACK
Submitted on 5/6/10
Red

December 25, 2009 (trippy manic flashback)

The sun roof was open and the winter air rushed in as we sped down Route 68 towards the next meeting place. It was Christmas night, and my journey was one from which storytellers will make their own legends. I was completely aware of my surroundings and had a connection that moved through my entire body as it revealed secrets hidden for generations. This mission had started yesterday morning on my drive up north to see my family. I was in possession of a secret that was meant to be the savior of mankind. It was I who had been chosen to complete the direst of missions, which I did not yet fully understand. The entire plan had been laid out before me in my mind, and while I knew what I had to do, actually doing it terrified and confused me.

I spun back to the previous morning in my mind as I lifted my hands through my open sunroof and clapped to the beat of the song. The colors all around me came alive in multidimensional ways. The hazards of a broken-down vehicle caught my eye, and the driver signaled me to slow down. A smile overtook my face. I could see the puzzle and mystery align before me, and I became engulfed in the game.

The cars' colors became a code on the Interstate. My "brother" blew his semi horn to alert me to evil, but I continued on my journey. My youngest brother's new dog was named Liberty; the subtle coincidences of everyday life began to take meaning. I took control of the situation and all hell broke loose . . .

TBC . . .

SESSION

DT: Wow, I was manic as shit right there; I was definitely in the spin.

JP: Yeah, there are the hallucinations, delusional thinking, thoughts of grandiosity, and a preoccupation with thought and schemes that may lead to self-neglect.

DT: Yeah, one hell of a ride, let me tell you.

KEY TERMS: ONIONS, ACCIDENTS, "USERS," SELFISHNESS
Submitted on 5/25/10
Red

January 1, 2010 (trippy manic flashback):
HAPPY NEW YEAR!!!!!!
WAHOOOOO!!!!!
AAAAAAHHHHHHHH!!!!
HAPPY 2010!!!!!!

A couple of the patients were running up and down the halls of our unit screaming and celebrating the New Year. I wasn't in the mood to celebrate. I rolled over on my side and tried to go back to sleep. Hopefully tomorrow I'd get out of the ward. Too bad that deep down, I knew that wasn't true.

I had gone to bed early, before any of the NYE parties had kicked off. I was still quite delusional; I believed that the television shows, especially football games, were being influenced by my thoughts. The weather for a majority of the bowl games was pretty awful, and I thought that was in direct relationship to my "attempt" to end the world. I spent most of my NYE sitting on a window sill, looking out the window and wondering what my friends were doing. I was sure they were excitedly preparing for the upcoming festivities: getting dressed up, buying booze, trying on their ridiculous 2010 framed glasses, and celebrating another year on the books. I, on the other hand, was lost and confused once again.

Stubby came by the hospital on New Year's Day and tried to lift my spirits by bringing me a pizza. He had accidentally put onions on it, and I cussed him out and walked out on him for it. It was taking every bit of my strength to battle my way back from my episode, and I felt like I couldn't get a break. Why were my parents and my aunt the only ones who had bothered to visit me in here?

Present Day:

A family friend recently had a horrible farming accident that threatened his life. It's almost scarily common for one of these accidents to occur in the community; that's part of the farming life. Stubby and I had just gotten to Chicago when we heard the news. We were provided with updates from our family, who had gone to the hospital to offer support. When Poncho was badly hurt in a snowmobile accident so many family members and friends came to console our family at the hospital. Almost no one came to see me on the psych ward.

In hindsight, it was probably better that my friends and family didn't visit me in the hospital; I know I wasn't a pretty sight. But at the time I felt bitter, sitting there alone in the psych ward on NYE, knowing that just about everyone I knew was out celebrating life while I was fighting for mine. Once I left the hospital, I struggled for a while with the notion that people didn't care. I've always thought as myself as a friend who is there in others' times of need, always willing to lend a hand and give encouragement. In my time of need, I felt betrayed by the self-ishness of others and the "users" I once thought as my friends.

To say I still don't struggle with this from time to time would be a lie. However, I've tried to use this struggle to motivate myself; to give me strength to be the person I know I can be rather the person I think everyone else wants me to be. I swore I would not speak to some friends who I felt had totally deserted me in my most vulnerable time, but that would make me no better than them.

SESSION

JP: The psych ward is not only an intimidating environment for patients, but also for friends and family. Not many of us enjoy being in hospitals; it reminds us of our mortality. When you combine that with mental health issues, it can exaggerate everything due to the vast unknowns involved. It may seem like betrayal or selfishness, but it's usually related to fear, anxiety, and intimida--"

♪♪ ♪♪♪

JP: What's that? Is that your ringtone?
DT: Oh hey, dude; no, I can talk . . .
JP: Rude.

KEY TERMS: HOT SHEETS, INTERNSHIP, SPORTS, CAREER
Submitted on 6/10/10
Red

June 8, 2010 (trippy manic flashback):
"Alright guys, I'm going to take it easy on you because you're all new and didn't know what you were doing, but these hot sheets . . ."

—My boss at my internship

I began to lose focus and started drifting away in my mind. My ability to stay in the now was slowly fading, and I started to separate from space and time. My heart rate slowed down at first and then steadily rose and fell, despite my efforts to control it. My arms began to tingle . . .

"Is this really happening now? Come on."

I tried to center myself and make eye contact and take notes, but the efforts were useless. A mellow energy overtook me and my hands became numb. I was using all my strength to maintain control, but I knew it was coming unless I did something.

Back at my desk, I had difficulty stopping the tears and blamed it on my allergies. I knew this wasn't going to work.

Present Day:
That's life and it's not fair
It is what it is
God works in mysterious ways
What does not kill me can only make me stronger
Everyone has problems
You can only play the hand you are dealt

I have been reciting these sayings over and over in my head for the past twenty-four hours or so to help myself deal with my latest BMD experience. I had to resign from my internship yesterday due to the feelings described in the above passage; my mania was coming back. I thought that if I entered into something that I loved, like sports, it would somehow counteract my mania and I'd be fine. Unfortunately, that is not the case, and now I've got to start from square one. Again.

I will be moving back to Ohio and more than likely The Nasty in August to try and figure out this BMD and how I can live with it. In a way, I'm actually looking forward to moving back because I never left out of spite or dislike but because I was chasing a dream. The dream of making it in the sports marketing industry, like the success I had found with AT&Tizzle before episode uno. That dream is gone now. I simply can't do it.

I love The Nasty and the people there, and it's home, but I am struggling with not being able to do things that once came easily to me. I thrived in the high-octane, fast-paced, high-stress sales environment of AT&Tizzle and thought if I only changed industries I'd be fine. That it was the telecommunications aspects of the previous job that had triggered my mania, and by following my passion in sports in the City of Wind I'd be fine. It's difficult to accept that something at which I once succeeded, something I enjoyed, something I was building my life around is gone forever.

BMD has made me take a look at my life. I feel as though I have nothing to show for my hard work, dedication and persistence. This feeling has drained me of energy to the point where I sit and cry, trying to understand something that is beyond my comprehension . . .

Keep faith and keep fighting

SESSION

JP: This one could almost be categorized with your depressed moods as well, don't you think?

DT: Yeah, without a doubt. That's the thing with my mania: at times it can throw me from one extreme to the next rather quickly. Just another example of the spin.

KEY TERMS: 911, "ELEMENTS," FANTASY, K. J. CHOI
Submitted on 6/29/10
Red

February 24 or so, 2008 (trippy manic flashback):

"In case of an emergency, please locate the nearest exit of the San Jose airport; or if you are in need of assistance, the nearest airport personnel. The following items are restricted . . ."

My phone started to vibrate in my pocket, and I began to sense something was wrong.

Unknown number.

"Hello?"

"911, what's your emergency?"

"Uh, well, I'm sorry, but I don't have an emergency. You called me."

"No, I'm sorry, sir, this call came to us. Is there anything you need assistance with at the airport?"

How did they know where I was? It must have been the surveillance cameras. This had to be a test of my nerves. I had been having trouble keeping my cool, and they must have seen me nervously pacing around.

"No problems here, ma'am. I didn't realize I had called you. My apologies."

"Well, you might have accidentally called us. Was your phone in your pocket?"

"Yes, it was in my front jacket pocket."

"Sometimes that happens. Have a good day."

"Thanks."

How did she know my phone was in my pocket? There was no way I accidentally called 911--my phone was locked. Why were they checking up on me? Did they think I couldn't handle this? *They* chose *me* to complete this mission, not the other way around. Remember to keep composure; balance, dedication, awareness and passion . . .

Present Day:

I'm still unclear if the above series of events were real or hallucinated while I was visiting San Jose during episode uno. At this point, I was pretty confused about what was real and what were fantasies. I also thought I met K. J. Choi in the airport, so your guess is as good as mine.

I realize that I've been complaining about my life a lot lately. My apologies for being selfish and not filling you in on other aspects of my episodes.

For instance, the four "elements" I listed above--balance, dedication, awareness and passion--played significant roles in episode uno. They make up the 4 in .e4. I became obsessed with these "elements" of my life and spent hours (if not days, I really couldn't tell you, I was pretty gone in the spin) writing them down in my gournal.

I was under the impression (though not too far off, I do believe) that the world (well, world = my life, one and the same during my episodes) was out of whack. That I was concentrating on the materials of my life rather than on what really mattered, like being dedicated to my passions while having balance throughout all aspects of my life, to bring me to awareness of everything around me. Looking back, maybe these elements really aren't so far off from reality; I just had to go crazy to realize that.

TBC . . .

SESSION

DT: Yeah, so I just recently heard K. J. Choi talk in an interview, and he definitely has a strong accent, which means I didn't meet him in the San Jose airport because the guy I met didn't have an accent. Which also means the phone call was more than likely not real, which means--

JP: You were extremely manic with hallucinations, delusions, and thoughts of grandiosity.

DT: Yeah, that sounds way better than batshit crazy like I was going to say. Thanks, JP.

KEY TERMS: PURGATORY, THE WARD, FORBIDDEN FRUIT, PARANOIAC

Submitted on 12/10/10
Red

December 29, 2009-January 4, 2010 (trippy manic flashback):

THE WARD

Forbidden Fruit

I took a bite of the apple, and suddenly the tastes of bleach and of poison filled my mouth. I took off in a sprint towards my bathroom. The toxic smell of poison filled my nostrils as I knelt over the toilet and profusely dry-heaved. I had hardly eaten in days, so each acid reflux was drier and drier until I was merely spitting out saliva. I had eaten the forbidden fruit, and this was my punishment.

I am in purgatory.

Paranoiac

I grabbed my wrist and felt around, anxiously trying to find a pulse, a beat, a sign of life, but nothing. I switched wrists and fumbled, trying desperately to find evidence that I existed. I grabbed the side of my neck below my jawline and squeezed slightly; I knew I'd find a beat here. After all those years checking my pulse in track, there was no way I'd have trouble feeling it in my neck; it was second nature. Nothing. I switched sides of my neck but to no avail. My legs were spread apart as I sat in my room, and the realization that all of this was not real started to creep into me. I frantically searched my chest for my heartbeat. Each second, the paranoia grew and grew.

I am in purgatory.

Judgment

"The judge won't be back until Monday. All the courts are closed."

What judge? I had admitted myself this time. There couldn't be a seventy-two-hour hold on me if I came in under my own free will. Wait; was it my own free will? Why did I have to see a judge if I'd done nothing wrong? Unless this was all real and I had started the apocalypse. Was this a test of my faith? I did nothing wrong.

I am in purgatory.

Innocent Scars

Such a pretty girl; I had to help . . .

"What are those on your arms?"

"Nothing."

"You shouldn't do that."

"Why does it matter?"

"It matters to your family."

"Yeah, I've been talking to them more lately."

"You should, they care."

I am in purgatory.

Together?

I was warned to stop socializing with the others. I seemed to be having a negative effect on one of the girls. It perplexed me, that by trying to help I could do so much harm. What place was I in when simply talking with someone jeopardized their wellbeing? I had only wanted to help others, and now it seemed I was the cause of such pain that she stiffened up and froze whenever I was around. I didn't understand how she could help me so much, yet when I tried to return the favor, I hurt her even more.

I am in purgatory.

Getting Back Up

"How do you feel?"

"Good, like I'm back."

"Well, you'll get your release today, and you do have someone to pick you up?"

"Yeah, my dad; the nurses told me this morning what time to have him come by."

"The hospital will be in touch with you, and the doctor in charge of the study will be reaching out to you as well, good luck."

I leave the ward.

SESSION

DT: Yep, reading that brought back some memories I haven't had in a while.

JP: Like what?

DT: Well, the girl who was frightened of me or whatever and one of the other girls wanted to watch a movie on New Year's Eve. We'd been watching football all week, and I'm pretty sure they were growing tired of it. They asked me if I could try to hook up the DVD player to the TV. The problem was, the remote was lost and the TV was behind a plastic shield, so I had to try and program everything using a pencil and pushing the buttons through holes in the shield. Quite a sight, let me tell you. I wanted to help and make the girls' night a little better, give them something to take their minds off the craziness in their lives. But I just couldn't do it. I tried forever but was just short a wire or something like that.

JP: I'm sorry that didn't work out for you, Derek.

DT: Yeah, me too, but I'll make it right one day.

KEY TERMS: A GIRL, MANIC LETTER, INSPIRE, INTERVENTION
Submitted on 1/28/11
Red

The past couple of weeks haven't been my best. I'm not sure if I'm in depression, still recovering from the Rockies, or if it's mania wreaking havoc on my life again. I try to stay optimistic and have a positive outlook during these bleak times, but it can be the most difficult thing to manage. Well, that and trying not to get caught staring at the slamming hot body trainer at the gym; oh yeah, she knows I'm looking. I try to remind myself of everything I do have when my mind gets trapped on what I don't. That I have it pretty good and there are a lot of people out there struggling more than me.

I wasn't quite sure if I'd ever share this story until a couple of days ago, mainly because it's not entirely my story to tell. There's a girl (when isn't there, right?), well, not any girl but my prom date (and maybe a little bit of a crush) from my junior year. This girl was smart, shockingly funny, a knockout who always smiled (even at my stupid poems, how do you think I asked her to prom?), and had the confidence to match that of yours truly. Years passed after school, and we went our separate ways until I became manic for the first time.

I caught her show one night, and the girl on TV was far from the one I could remember from high school. She was in the fight of her life, she was in hell . . .

February 24, 2008 (trippy manic flashback):
Friends,

Some of you know me, but I imagine the majority of you do knot . . . it makes really no difference as I am of no significance for the purpose of this letter aside from the hope that it may prove to provide some help some way some day . . . I am sitting in the San Jose's AIR awaiting my flite back to Denver, CO and decided to jot some ideas down, as I await the arrival of our plane . . . While I live in Denver I am originally from a small town in rural Ohio by the name of South Charleston (yes I do mean OH and not SC, WV or any other of the multiple "Charlestons" throughout) . . . I am riting now as it has become clear to me how fortunate I, as well as many of us, are . . . yet it seems as fortunate as we are we miss out on the important things in life . . . what those are to you, the gentleman beside me or the cowgirl? (tough to differentiate from afar) sitting across the way are I don't know . . . but I know I am missing . . . Live downtown Denver in a pretty nice apt, recently purchased a BMW X5, amazing friends, and a great family . . . please know I am not writing this to impress anyone, but rather to hopefully inspire someone . . .

Inspiration is a word that I believe many of us struggle with . . . I have had the ultimate opp. 2 travel around the globe for work, play, and study . . . however even with my experiences I still lacked something . . . what that is I could not say till now . . . not cuz I did not want to, but rather b/c I did not know . . . the past few days have been pretty damn exciting for me . . . I am moving from Denver 2 CA for a new job opp. I have been working 3 yrs to achieve and now! get to finally live w/in an hour of a beach . . . while this may seem modest to some pls realize that central OH is not the ideal place for h2o sports . . .

Looking back on the times and trials that have brought me to this place I could BORE many for hours over my experiences, but what's the point? Who has not felt pain, joy, fear, pleasure, disappointment, jealously, rage, excitement, enthusiasm, ect . . . I have yet to meet anyone along my way that has not . . . but what I have found is that my fondest memories are the ones in Kindergarten (my 2nd time, they redshirted me my 1st yr) . . . the values and colors I experienced came rushing back to me . . . now reflecting back I wish it didn't take 2X for me to get thru kindergarten, I wish I was still there . . .

Well we all know that's impossible (unless you're a kindergarten cop or teacher) . . . while I've contemplated both these options, they just didn't fit me . . . so I've decided to try and change . . .

Internvention TV Show: "(Radio Edit) Episode XX--(Radio Edit), XX, grew up struggling to meet her parents' high expectations. Despite winning many academic and athletic honors,

(Radio Edit) suffered from depression and low self-esteem, and her shameful feelings intensified when she became a date-rape victim in college. She dieted in hopes of regaining control of her emotions and life, but now she weighs less than 90 pounds. Her family's last hope is an intervention that will stop her from starving herself to death."

I had the pleasure of escorting this young lady to her Sr. Prom (my Jr yr, remember redshirt Kindergarten) . . . I started to remember what a great time we <u>all</u> had at the Prom (Prom promise that) and seeing how she and her fam are now hurts and I want to help . . . but how? . . . no idea right now, but maybe, just maybe, showing that we care is a start . . .

Present Day:
I didn't sign this letter but instead started doodling .e4 logos and missions statements. Oh, d01roK, you crazy guy, you. Less than a week after writing this letter in my gournal, I was in Porter Hospital's psych ward. I've been able to catch up with (Radio Edit) and actually got to spend Halloween hanging out; seems a fitting holiday for us two to share. I haven't talked to her in a while, and I hope she's doing alright. She's about the only one I know who can kind of relate to me, and I hope she knows I still see the same girl I crushed on in high school.

SESSION
JP: Your manic letter is interesting. What made you think of writing it when you were in your episode? And do your more affectionate feelings always seem to rise during this state?

DT: Well, I caught the show one night in Denver during my episode, which is probably why she was in my head at this point and probably the reason for the letter. To answer your second question, I would definitely say I am more affectionate during my manic episodes; those feelings seem to drive me. I'm more affectionate towards women, all the women I know and strangers on the street. I also seem to take a defensive stance towards men while manic.

JP: Do you have any idea why you would take this approach towards women?

DT: Yep, I love 'em, and my mania knows that.

KEY TERMS: FINE LINE
Submitted on 5/26/11
Red

Fine Line

I've heard there's a fine line between genius and madness
But the thing about my madness is that it feels just like brilliance
So I guess that's the genius of the complexity in all of this
Having me walk a fine line that I'm not quite sure exists
Am I really that mad or just ahead of all the rest

At times I can get confused about the difference between madness and genius
Like if genius is showing the world something new that it has never experienced
Taking that which had only been known as false and turning it into fact
If that's the case then my crazy madness they call mania is exactly that
This maddening mania of mine takes control of me and won't give it back

---

It takes me into the spin where my world becomes manically unhinged
Making me follow maddening clues in my head that I'm unable to comprehend
Taking me on a journey of enlightenment that seemingly has no beginning or end
Where the madness reveals the brilliance in everything all around
Allowing for the genius of the simplicity in it all to be found
Like walking on both sides of an imaginary fine line on the ground

---

I've heard there's a fine line between genius and madness
Now you've seen how my madness can feel just like brilliance
How there is genius in the complexity of the simplicity within all of this
Having us all walk that fine line that I'm not quite sure exists
Am I really that mad or just like all of the rest

SESSION

JP: Did you know that in the 1970s, Kay Redfield Jamison studied forty-seven British writers, painters and sculptors from the Royal Academy? She found that 38 percent had been treated for bipolar disorder. Half of the poets--the largest group with manic depression--had needed medication or hospitalization. Interesting coincidence here, wouldn't you say?

DT: I happen to believe that the best ride you can give someone is to make them think differently about something. So thanks for the ride, JP.

JP: Anytime, my friend, anytime.

CONCLUSION

SESSION

JP: My diagnosis is that you are bipolar as shit, my friend.

DT: Ha-ha, just as I suspected. Thanks for reading.

JP: Whoa, whoa mister. You don't think you're getting off that easy, do you? Answering a few more questions about your life to fill in the blanks for the readers is the least you can do, don't you think?

DT: You can't get enough of me, can you? That's precious.

JP: OK, so our confidence is still high. Has that led to any progress in the love department?

DT: I'm ambidextrous now if that's what you mean.

JP: Still single, I see but have you at least been trying to date?

DT: When I was living in The Nasty about a year ago I did try to date but it just didn't work. I think I was still trying to find myself with this BMD so it was difficult to date someone when I really didn't know who I was. Since then I've moved out into the country in one of our small family farm houses where the nearest civilization has a population of around 400, so the pickings are slim. I'm ready to date but haven't had much luck so I've even tried the online scene with Match.com, and failed miserably. Wow, I'm really glad we could talk about this because it's not making me feel pathetic or anything.

JP: Ok, maybe you've had better luck in the career department?

DT: Well, let's see. I recently dropped out of graduate school to basically write this book. I have a single course and an internship left until I can receive my master's in sports administration at Xavier University. We'll see how that decision works out.

JP: With such a small portion of your degree left to complete would you consider going back to finish the masters? It is quite an impressive achievement for anyone, let alone someone fighting something as difficult as bipolar disorder.

DT: I'd like to think I will go back and finish at some point but I'll have to wait and see. I dropped out because I wasn't sure what I wanted to do with my life and I was having some trouble with symptoms of my mania again in Chicago and at Xavier. It's become quite evident that corporate America is a trigger for me from my past problems so that really limits what I can do. This is especially frustrating since my skill set is focused around corporate America. I still have till 2014 to finish my degree though, but I mean the world is supposed to end next year anyways.

JP: Oh yea, of course I forgot, well let's say the Mayans are misunderstood and we somehow survive. What's your plan for the next few years?

DT: I don't really know. I have had problems in the past with planning out these elaborate and detailed plans in my head for my future and then I seem to get ahead of myself. I build up my confidence too much and when things don't work out just like I planned I take it pretty tough on myself. These failed plans in the past have included going back into the telecommunication industry after episode uno, going back to school to get my masters, moving to Chicago to try and start a career in sports marketing only a few months after episode deuce, and then trying a traveling sales job close to home. And you know what? I've pretty much fell on my face after each and every one of them and I'm not going to lie, it doesn't feel good. So I've decided that I'm not going to worry about the future as much, I'm going to try and enjoy the ride, see what happens, and stay healthy.

JP: So does that mean that you're not working now?

DT: Actually, once again my support system comes through huge and my cousin helped me out with a job. I'm doing asphalt work like I did in college during the summers.

JP: How come you've never told me about this asphalt/construction crew of yours?

DT: Because I didn't trust you around the guys, honestly I've been around you at construction sites and it can be embarrassing.

JP: Even with that untruthful and unnecessary shot at me I'm going to say I'm still very impressed with all you've accomplished over the past three years. You sound frustrated with your perception that you've failed at all these things you listed.

But you've managed to accomplish more than a lot of people would be able to without having to deal with a life-challenging illness such as bipolar disorder. Lighten up on yourself bud, but I do also want to know if your family and friends were supportive of these decisions, including dropping out to write a book?

DT: Most of them laugh and shake their heads, knowing that's just the new me now living with the BMD the best I can. I usually don't tell or discuss things all that much until I've made a decision. It's pretty selfish of me I know, but it's just the way I've approached my life. Stubborn and hard headed to the point that I believe I can do basically anything I put my mind to. My family understands that because; well, because I had to get it from somewhere I guess. I think they just want me to be happy and to stay the fuck out of the hospital. But in all seriousness, I couldn't ask for a better support system. I am very fortunate to have these people in my life. I hope I make them proud with all my craziness.

JP: I love your family.

DT: Yeah, I know, JP. You're like at all our family functions now.

JP: That reminds me, we're having a cookout next weekend for your aunt's birthday.

DT: Unbelievable. Can we get to the next question?

JP: How about your health, how's everything going with that?

DT: Good. I've been on lithium since November of 2010 and it seems to be working for me, and I'm feeling much more like myself now than at any other time in the past three years.

JP: Does that mean you haven't had any manic episodes or depressive periods as of late?

DT: Thankfully on the manic side I haven't had any episodes since episode deuce in late December of 2009. I have had some close calls in Chicago and then down in Nashville but luckily I was able to separate myself from the triggers before things got crazy, literally.

JP: What were those triggers?

DT: Um, mostly just the work environment. Both instances I was trying to get my career back in a high pressure stress environment, similar to the one I excelled in at AT&T, but I can't do it anymore. That usually sends me into depression that lasts a couple months. I've been in a depressed state about four times since episode deuce. But I think if I can get through this winter without another manic episode, I'll be pretty confident we've got the medication right. I'll have to wait and see, but I'm optimistic about my health in the future.

JP: We? So I take it things are going smoothly with the new docs?

DT: Well, I did find a place in The Nasty through my insurance that practices with two docs. One is a psychiatrist who prescribes the lithium for me and another who's my counselor and more of a therapist role. I don't really argue with these docs but I don't entirely trust them either. I started out liking my counselor but that relationship has begun to go south. I feel like he's disengaged after only about four visits with me over the last eight months. I was never a fan of the psychiatrist but I can manage her. They're just nothing like you JP.

JP: Fair enough, that certainly made up for the earlier smart-ass remark. The important things are to remain on your medication and keep an open dialogue with your support system.

DT: Yep. Now, is there any other question that makes you feel like you can't live without the answer, JP?

JP: Just one more. Can you tell the readers what I caught you looking up on the Internet yesterday evening?

DT: Oh, you DICK! You said you wouldn't say anything. I was just curious about how one would go about pulling off a sex position like that!

Acknowledgements

I couldn't have done any of this without all you haters out there. If it wasn't for your complete and utter lack of faith in not only me, but also this entire project, then none of this would have been possible. Your tireless and relentless verbal assaults on my character and the idea behind this book is what pushed me to work so much harder.

Thanks haters, I owe you one!

References
(Double check me haters.)

About.com. Bipolar Disorder. 10 April 2011. <http:// http://bipolar.about.com/>

Bipolar Central: Devoted to Helping Those Living with Bipolar Disorder. 10 April 2011. <http:// www.bipolarcentral.com/>

bp magazine. 3 March 2011. <http://www. http://bphope.com/>

Depression and Bipolar Support Allicance. 24 February 2011. <http://http://www.dbsalliance.org/site/PageServer?pagename=home>

Drugs.com: Drug Information Online. 25 March 2011. <http:// http://www.drugs.com/>

Drugs.com. 12 March 2011 < http://www.drugs.com/sfx/lithium-carbonate-side-effects.html>

Mayo Clinic. 25 March 2011 <http:// http://www.mayoclinic.com/>

National Alliance on Mental Illness. 3 March 2011. <http://www. http://nami.org/>

National Institutes of Health. 25 April 2011. < http://www.nih.gov/>

National Institute of National Health. 25 April 2011. <http:www. http://www.nimh.nih.gov/index.shtml>

Think Exist: Finding Quotations was never this Easy!. 24 February 2011. <http://www. http://thinkexist.com/>

Made in the USA
Charleston, SC
25 May 2012